The Puerto Ricans

CHRISTOPHER

The Puerto Ricans

RAND

OXFORD UNIVERSITY PRESS

New York

© 1958 by Christopher Rand
Library of Congress Catalogue Card Number: 58-10733
First published, 1958
This reprint, 1971
Printed in the United States of America

Most of the material in this book appeared originally
in *The New Yorker* in somewhat different form;
© 1957 The New Yorker Magazine, Inc.

F
128.9
.P8
R3

PSYCHO

The translations of songs from "Neuva York," a tape
documentary by Tony Schwartz,
are used with the permission of Folkways Records.

75625

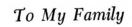

To My Family

Acknowledgment

This whole work was undertaken by the New Yorker *and me together, and without the* New Yorker *it would not have been done.*

I have also been helped by innumerable people in or near the Puerto Rican community of New York. I could not list them all, and it might embarrass them anyway, for many Puerto Ricans dislike having their affairs discussed with outsiders. So I shall not mention these helpers, but they know what they did for me, and I trust they know how I thank them.

C. R.

Contents

The Puerto Ricans

I *El Barrio de Nueva York*

Some 550,000 Puerto Ricans were living in New York at the start of 1957—a fourteenth, more or less, of the city's population. Nearly all of them had arrived in the preceding ten years, though a slight trickle had been coming in earlier: roughly speaking since 1898, the year we took their island from Spain. The first Puerto Ricans to move north were cigar makers, merchant seamen, and women garment workers, and they concentrated in three spots: on Sands Street in Brooklyn and on 99th and 135th Streets in Harlem. These communities were tiny. A Puerto Rican cigar maker who came up in 1921 has told me that they numbered only a few hundred people then between them, and that he soon knew almost all the two hundred personally. It was not till the late 'twenties that the Puerto Ricans began giving a really Spanish flavor to East Harlem, and not till the 'thirties that they called that region El Barrio, or El Barrio de Nueva York—*barrio* is a Spanish word meaning village, locality, or ward. East Harlem is still called El Barrio, and it is the main Puerto Rican focus in the city, though by no means the only one.

El Barrio's center might be placed at the 110th Street subway station of the Lexington Avenue line, an establishment whose lavatories bear the words HOMBRES and MUJERES on their doors, as well as MEN and WOMEN. If you ascend to daylight from that station you can expect to see Puerto Ricans on every hand, and you may well see no one else. El Barrio's southern edge is ragged, tending to stop a little below 100th Street, and the district has other irregularities too—notably a big Italian enclave near the East River around 116th Street. Yet this enclave, though prosperous and stoutly defended, has been shrinking, for many young Italians have left it since their broadening experiences in World War II. And Puerto Ricans have come in to fill the vacuum behind them.

On the southwest El Barrio touches Central Park. On the north it fades away toward the Harlem River, and on the west and northwest it yields to what is often called Central Harlem now: the area north of the Park, that is, between Fifth and Eighth Avenues. Terms like Central Harlem are not very stable. "Place-names in New York are not fixed items," a city planner explained to me recently. "Rather, the people carry them about on their backs. In the 'thirties we had a slump; few Negroes were coming to the city; and Harlem remained a fairly small place. But then the War, with its demand for labor, brought many new Negroes in, and Harlem spread. As it did so, the need to subdivide it was naturally felt, and you got an emphasis on the ideas of East, Central, and West Harlem."

Puerto Ricans are scanty in Central Harlem, but recur again, if patchily, in West Harlem, a district that, as many feel, goes right to the banks of the Hudson now, at least in places. Some leaders of the Hudson River neighborhoods are fighting this westward semantic drift of Harlem, as they want their old place-names, like Morningside Heights, Washington Heights, and Manhattanville, to survive, with their different connotations. How they will make out we cannot tell, but meanwhile if we see Harlem as an island-wide band—albeit a spotty, interrupted one—somewhere above 100th Street, we can say that Puerto Ricans occur in many parts of it, and that East Harlem is their part *par excellence*.

On Manhattan's West Side, Puerto Ricans can be found almost continually from "Harlem" down to the Chelsea District, in the twenties. But almost nowhere in that distance do their holdings make a solid extensive patch. This is especially true above 59th Street, where the north-south arteries—like Central Park West, Broadway, West End Avenue, and Riverside Drive—are so often lined with big apartment houses. The Puerto Ricans have not moved into these, by and large, but have made strong inroads on the sidestreet brownstones between them, taking these over from their earlier occupants—often Irish-Americans—cutting them up into tiny rooms or apartments, overcrowding them, and helping to run them down. Thus they have been giving the West Side population a laminated quality, where slums or near-slums are interleaved with homes of the middle class.

It is a condition unique among the city's Puerto Rican districts, which otherwise tend to be slums pure and simple, shared with Negroes or the less mobile remnants of European immigrant groups, and it makes for a tricky problem of adjustment. Many of the West Side middle-class families have traditionally believed in sending their children to public schools and raising them without class distinction, but the Puerto Rican influx has tried their resolve severely. A high percentage of Puerto Ricans in a school drags the teaching down almost inevitably, because of the language problem, and when Puerto Rican children are in a majority on a street they can, like any such majority, make life almost unbearable for other children. Faced with these facts of life, the richer West Side "men of good will," as they might call themselves, have often reluctantly sent their children to private schools (which are now booming in that region) or moved off to the suburbs. Those who remain may try to mix with their new neighbors in the P.T.A. and other bodies, but they find this difficult. The two groups can hardly, for instance, invite each other to refreshments with much ease, so great is the gulf between their respective customs and living standards.

These sharp contrasts occur on the Upper West Side—above, say, the fifties—rather than the Lower, for sections like Hell's Kitchen and Chelsea tend to be slums unmixed again, or mixed chiefly with industrial islands, like the garment district. The Puerto Ricans have been moving to these latter places in the past few years, though not without objection from the older residents there—Chelsea, for instance, had an anti-Puerto Rican riot in the hot weather of 1949.

Below Chelsea the Puerto Ricans die out; they are not noticeable in Greenwich Village, or eastward to the Bowery. Across that line, though, they recur again intensely, in New York's classic slum, and classic beachhead for newcomers, the Lower East Side. Here they have moved in, along with Negroes, for the past five years or so, increasing all the time in number and replacing the older immigrants—especially Jews and Italians—who have been moving to the suburbs or the country. The Italians have usually moved out bag and baggage, but often the Jews have kept their shops going behind them, merely changing their lines of merchandise to suit the new customers, and hiring Puerto Rican salesmen or learning Spanish themselves. On the sidewalk stalls of Orchard Street now, you may find bright Catholic images for sale, perhaps with Spanish words on them like *Dios Bendiga Nuestro Hogar*—"God Bless Our Home." The big shops of Delancey Street, the Fifth Avenue of that quarter, are still Jewish, but Spanish words are creeping into their signs; the word SHOES, for instance, may have ZAPATOS, its Spanish equivalent, printed beneath it. The Jewish shopkeepers linger on in the field of general merchandise and in the more expensive locations, but Puerto Ricans themselves are running most of the *bodegas,* the little Spanish-American food shops, on the side streets. In this they show a commercial bent, incidentally, that is not shared by the Negroes, a group that coincides with them in certain other ways. The Negroes rarely keep shops in New York, and in some places the Puerto Ricans do it for them.

The slums are full of cosmopolitan juxtapositions like this, and none is more so than the Lower East Side. In the early nineteenth century that region was a rustic suburb for well-to-do Anglo-Saxons, and the streets there got Anglo-Saxon names by and large. Stanton and Rivington Streets were named for Tory sympathizers. Chrystie, Forsyth, Eldridge, Ludlow, and Allen Streets were named for heroes of the War of 1812. It was soon after that war that Irish immigrants began pouring in there. They were followed by immigrants from Germany, Italy, and countless parts of Central Europe; and even today there are said to be twenty-seven different nationalities in the district. The inflow stopped in the 'twenties, but the more static of the immigrants have remained there since then, enjoying fame as a social phenomenon and receiving much attention from settlement houses and other agencies of uplift; I have been told that more charitable aid goes to the Lower East Side than to any other comparable place in the world. Now that the Puerto Ricans have entered this great antechamber, of course, they are getting much of the aid themselves. The settlement houses have stirred to new life at their coming, and a demand has arisen for Spanish-speaking social workers.

Outside Manhattan, there are many Puerto Ricans in the South Bronx, where they have been entrenched for years.

There are many in Brooklyn too. There are few in Queens so far, but there are many in New Jersey, in Suffolk County, Long Island, and in other light industrial centers of the Northeast, including cities like Bridgeport and Rochester. Often they go even as far west as Chicago, where there were twenty-five thousand of them at last report.

But New York is their main goal. It is the place they think of in Puerto Rico when they think of the great world. It is where the ships used to bring them and where the planes bring them now. The Puerto Rican government encourages them to fan out in their migration and not to pile up in the city; but to the extent they do this they fan mainly to New York's hinterland—since the West is far away, and Dixie is seldom considered because of segregation. Many of those who stop in New York return to their island, too, sooner or later, or send their children back in the school vacations; their migration is not the sheer uprooting that the European immigrants went through.

There is reason to believe, furthermore, that Puerto Ricans are quite mobile within New York itself. This is less true of those in El Barrio, perhaps, where there is a relatively long Puerto Rican tradition, and more true of those, say, on the Lower East Side, where conditions are bad and where new housing projects keep stirring things up. Almost any slum-clearance venture is apt to hurt the Puerto Ricans, temporarily at least, instead of helping them, as it obliterates the worst old tenements and forces them to move on elsewhere. In general the Puerto Ricans on the Lower East Side do not stay put long, and they include a high percentage of newcomers fresh off the plane, many of these being *jíbaros*, or hillbillies from the country districts of the island —people not used to city life at all.

Usually New York's Puerto Ricans concentrate most

heavily in old slums or "changing neighborhoods" ready to become slums, and it helps if these are handy to one or more subways—subways being the Puerto Rican lifelines, as late-afternoon travelers on the IRT need not be told. The Puerto Rican government maintains an office in New York to watch over the migration and to help find jobs and solve problems for the thousands of migrants who turn to it each month. Up to now the office has been located at Columbus Avenue near Broadway, about six blocks from Columbus Circle. This is an ideal spot because the IRT, BMT, and Independent systems all pass within five or ten minutes' walk of it, and the bus terminals for Jersey and upstate New York are not too far away. But that building is soon to be torn down, as part of the Lincoln Square renovation scheme, and the migrant office is hard pressed to find anything half so central to the peculiar world it serves.

A great deal is heard about Puerto Ricans on relief in New York, and this is something we can return to later. It is true that the number of them on relief, in proportion, is slightly greater than that of New York residents as a whole—much relief, especially, goes to unwed Puerto Rican mothers with broods of little children. But nearly all those close to the subject deny that Puerto Ricans come here with relief as their objective. They come to get jobs or to join their near and dear ones, these experts say, and the relief is something they fall into later.

On the job-ladder the Puerto Ricans share the lower rungs with the Negroes, but do not share them equally. The Negroes have a slight advantage in most lines, because of language and because they have been here longer. This does not apply to the garment trade, though, where Puerto

Rican women are in great demand. Puerto Rico has an old tradition of fine needlework, and Puerto Ricans are also rated high in both "manual" and "finger" dexterity. The International Ladies' Garment Workers' Union has about forty thousand "Spanish-speaking" members in the city—the bulk of these are Puerto Ricans, but they prefer to be lumped with Cubans, South Americans, and other Latins as "Spanish-speaking," which is thought a less derogatory term in New York now. The Spanish-speakers make up almost a fifth of the ILGWU's New York City membership, and one hears that the garment industry would be in a bad way without them. In some shops of the garment district you can find solid rows of Puerto Rican women, all behind their sewing machines and talking Spanish as they slide the dresses through. You can find Puerto Rican men in those shops too, and in many other of the light New York manufacturing plants. Recently I have visited a foam-rubber plant, an aquarium-supply house, and a corrugated-box factory within the New York City limits, all of which had many Puerto Rican workers. There seems, in fact, to be an affinity between New York, the Puerto Rican influx, and this kind of off-beat light industry.

Many Puerto Ricans also work at assembling TV and electronic equipment in New York and nearby cities. Many are messenger-boys. And of course many work in hotels and restaurants, chiefly in the lower jobs like those of busboy, dishwasher, or vegetable man, though they can rise a good deal higher if they learn English and are determined. The Hilton and Sheraton hotels in New York employ hundreds of Puerto Ricans, and, like the garment trade, would be in a bad way without them.

Yet the number of New York Puerto Ricans in domestic service is negligible, though many of the city's Negroes are in such work. Language often bars Puerto Ricans from domestic jobs, of course. So does the fact that their women often have several knee-high children of their own to take care of. Finally, there is a tradition in Puerto Rico against doing domestic work for pay. The family in Puerto Rico is thought of as extensive, with cousins at some remove being included. A rich household, therefore, is apt to take in the children of poor cousins, educate them a little, and work them in the kitchen while treating them as relatives, not menials. This background is very different, of course, from that of the Negroes in our South.

There are some two thousand Puerto Rican civil servants in New York, with an association of their own. Many of them are mail-carriers and the most august of them, perhaps, is a ship's architect in the Brooklyn Navy Yard. Early in 1957 I went to the association's yearly installation of officers, which was held in Hunts Point Palace, a big building in the Bronx that had been used for Jewish weddings and like festivities in the decades gone by. When I arrived, the more formal part of the meeting, including the speeches, was over, and the members and their wives were gathering in a ballroom to dance the dances, like the *merengue* and the *cha-cha-cha*, that Puerto Ricans go in for. The company was middle-aged and sedate, and soberly dressed in white-collar garb, yet one and all danced with abandon and gaiety, as I have seen Puerto Ricans doing at get-togethers of virtually all ages in the past few months. They are a dancing people.

Few Puerto Ricans have climbed to much real eminence in New York yet. There is one Tammany district leader (Antonio Mendez), one State assemblyman (Felipe N. Torres), and one municipal judge (Magistrate Manuel A. Gomez). Aside from these, the Puerto Rican community on the mainland, being so new and formless, has not thrown up many leaders of its own; and it is sometimes criticized for this in civic circles. There are other famous Puerto Ricans in the States, it is true—José Ferrer, the movie actor, is perhaps the best known of them. Such people do not come from the New York migrants, though, but from a small upper class in Puerto Rico, whose sons go to Ivy League colleges. There have also been some Puerto Rican athletes of note here. Pitcher Ruben Gomez of the Giants is one. Sixto Escobar, the great bantam-weight of yesteryear, was another. Many Puerto Ricans, indeed, have gone into prize-fighting, which has long been an escape route for the poor and underprivileged in this country.

Related to it, perhaps, is military service, and many Puerto Ricans have enlisted in our armed forces, where the pay looks bigger to them than to us mainlanders. Until recently our army had one wholly Puerto Rican regiment, the Sixty-fifth, which I remember visiting for a few days in Korea in 1951. Its Puerto Rican GIs didn't speak English too well and were rated less than perfect with modern weapons; but their courage, and ability to get round in the Korean hills, was much respected. A while ago the Sixty-fifth was de-activated, and now the Puerto Ricans who join up are put into our common basic-training pool on the mainland (after an eight-week tour of special instruction, mainly in English, at Fort Buchanan on their island).

One class of Puerto Rican migrants goes right through New York City—or right through Idlewild—after flying up here. These are contract workers who have been picked out by the Puerto Rican government for special jobs, mainly in agriculture. As a rule they start coming in late spring, when their own sugar harvest is over, and they may stay on till December, if they can get supplied with warm clothes. They sometimes take home a thousand dollars in pay after a season, and they are said to average $450. They pick things like fruit or cranberries, or they work in the Jersey truck gardens—it is said that many of them are settling now in South Jersey, as year-round truck-garden laborers. A new community, or *barrio*, of Puerto Rican chicken-farmers is also reported in New Jersey, near Lakewood. By and large, Puerto Ricans are adaptable, and they are likely to do whatever is offered. One thing they seem to do rarely, though, is to take farm jobs singly, on their own. They are gregarious and used to living in big family groups in crowded circumstances. Our mainland atmosphere strikes them as cold at best, physically and temperamentally, and they avoid getting isolated in it.

There is a good deal of Indian blood, along with European and African, among the Puerto Ricans. They run almost the full color gamut, from dark Negro to fair, though few of them have really tow heads or light-blue eyes. They have produced some special types—including the *indio*, which has copper skin and sometimes high cheekbones, and the *grifo*, which has fair skin but kinky hair or some other non-European feature. The various non-European types, including the Negro, make up a high percentage of the crowds one sees in the Puerto Rican ghettos here—higher, perhaps, than the percentage of such types in the city's over-all Puerto Rican population, as they are the ones who find it hardest to leave the ghettos and be assimilated.

Yet racial type is scarcely the most striking thing in New York's Puerto Rican scenes. Most striking is the dress—especially the dress of the women. Their styles come from Spanish antecedents and are radically different from those of mainland women, white or Negro. In fact, one can often spot a Puerto Rican woman a block away by the clothes she wears, and by their movement as she walks. The chief point is that her dress or skirt will be gathered tightly at the waist and will flare out wide toward the hem. Then as she steps along, inevitably with a free hip movement, the hem will swish considerably, clockwise and back again. Puerto Rican women also like scarves over their heads, in light colors that might be called pastel tones except that they usually have a metallic, or aniline-dye, look to them. The scarf-headed women—short, with their square shoulders, trim waists, and swishing hems—are a common sight in any Puerto Rican neighborhood, and so are the little girls who are their junior counterparts. These wear scarves too, and in the winter they may wear flaring overcoats in bright blue, pink, or green. Unless their families are very poor they are apt to be neat-looking, with clean white socks and clean shoes. If they can afford it they wear bits of jewelry—anything with color, anything gold or shiny—and as a rule their ears are pierced when they are young. After three o'clock, when the public schools let out, these little girls can be met sweeping along the sidewalks in yard-high floods, smelling faintly of bubble-gum and emitting a soprano babble in Spanish.

The men are less colorful, sartorially. In cold weather, indeed, they often wear U.S. Army surplus clothing, which gives them an over-all drab and brownish tone. The boys go in for an Elvis Presley mode, which blends well with their native island style—for curly duck-tailed hair, that is, with sideburns, and for blue jeans and black-leather or colored jackets.

On the Lower East Side one often sees Puerto Rican boys in leather jackets with nickel stars on their shoulders, as if they were generals. These jackets can be bought on Orchard

Street for about fifteen dollars. The colored cloth ones cost a few dollars more. They are usually made to order, in special colors and with special names on the backs, for clubs, baseball teams, and the like, and one hears that they are a mainstay of the gangs to which Puerto Rican and other slum boys belong. "The gangs might even go out of existence," a priest on the Lower East Side has told me, "if their members couldn't buy those jackets in special colors." The jackets make the boys feel tough—"feel almost like hoods," as another slum priest has put it—and give them a sense of solidarity.

These feelings of toughness and solidarity appear to be needed by many young Puerto Ricans now, when they have moved to the big, lonely city from their sunny isle, with its family and village relationships. A boy's jacket fills such needs symbolically, and it is often a burning question whether he will get it from gang activities or from sports.

In warm weather New York's Puerto Ricans are out of doors and in the streets. Those in their prime, of an evening, may be having a party and drinking beer, from cans. The older ones may be sitting apart playing dominoes, while the children play stickball and other street games. In such weather Nueva York offers a relatively full life to the Puerto Rican visitors. But in the cold it is different. Then they are driven back into their tenements, to huddle round unsafe kerosene stoves, and the landscape does without them in the main.

Before dawn on a winter morning not long ago, when it was snowing hard, I went down to the Lower East Side and witnessed scenes there that were both very beautiful and very bereft of Puerto Rican life, by normal standards. I got there before seven, and the streets were snow-padded and almost silent, though occasionally, while walking along, I heard the grate of a snow-shovel or the spatter of a truck in slush. Once I heard a cat whimper in a doorway. The snowflakes shone in the light of the street lamps.

Few people were about when I first got there, and almost none of them were Puerto Ricans. Mostly they seemed to be old European immigrants, and I felt they had been brought out by a landlord's duty to clear the sidewalks, as well as by their hardihood. In a couple of places I found two or three men gathered round garbage pails from which the flames of bonfires were rising, but these were not Puerto Ricans either. I met a few Puerto Rican men in time, but they hurried by me and were bundled up—a typical outfit might include a cap, earmuffs, high boots or galoshes, and a jacket with a synthetic-fleece collar. A few Puerto Rican women who hurried by were bundled up too and wore their head-scarves, though the colors didn't show in the gray storm. After wandering for some time I got cold myself and went off for a cup of coffee. When I returned it was about eight o'clock, and more and more Puerto Ricans, men and women, were emerging from the doorways, perhaps with their lunches in paper bags. They did not linger, but hurried away. After eight the Puerto Rican school children began to appear, bundled up of course, and carrying books and lunches. The boys experimented with snowballs, though the snow was really too dry for it.

By this time it was full daylight; yet the air was thick with snow-flurry and looked as if it would stay that way, so I joined a stream of adult Puerto Ricans and left the scene with them. They descended to the Independent station at Delancey Street and joined the age-old pack in the subway, to which they added not a little.

In the next week or two I visited several Puerto Rican slum dwellings, chiefly in East Harlem and Chelsea (I was taken by social workers or public-health nurses who knew the people there, for it seemed tactless to barge in on my own). Usually the halls were frigid in the tenements we went to, but the rooms themselves were warm—their windows were shut tight, and often the cracks round them were stuffed with paper. One or more burners of the place's gas range would be turned on, with the flame standing high, and if there was no central heating—as was often the case—an oil or kerosene stove might be burning away too. The air would be close, scented with fumes of the gas or oil, and with a characteristic rather sour cooking smell, which one nurse told me came from vegetable oil kept standing and used again and again in frying. There seemed often to be a fire-hazard in these rooms, and an asphyxiation-hazard too, and later in the winter I read from time to time, in the New York Spanish press, of asphyxiation cases or near escapes.

Yet short of catastrophes like this, the atmosphere in the rooms seemed as if it might prove cosy if one got used to the smells, and in many of them I saw little children going happily about half naked. Sometimes, I gathered, these children stayed home for days or even weeks on end, lacking the clothes and the inclination to brave the streets; and the mothers must have stayed home a lot too, watching them—in winter I suspect, indeed, that many New York Puerto Ricans stay cooped up entirely, taking no part in school or work or in the city's life.

Most of the flats or rooms I saw were crowded. A family of five might well be living in a single room, perhaps with a curtain hung across to divide it. They might be paying high rent too, say fifteen or twenty dollars a week, even though they had to share a kitchen and bathroom, in the hall, with neighboring families. Many rooms had no hot water, and a mother would have to cook some up to bathe her baby (a matter of concern to my guiding nurses). Even the poorest rooms, on the other hand, might have modern appliances—most likely an electric ice-box; more rarely a washing-machine; almost always a small radio; and quite commonly a TV set. An apartment might be tidy or slovenly, depending, I suppose, on the nature of the housewife. If it was tidy there might be special attempts at decoration in it, like curtains, pictures, and little paint jobs here and there, almost always in bright colors. In nearly every place I visited there were bright religious images, too, mainly of Christ and the Virgin.

Many dwellings were said to be infested with vermin: with rats, cockroaches, and bedbugs—or *ratas, cucarachas,* and *chinches,* as they were more familiarly known to the inhabitants. Cockroaches were the only ones of these I saw —on walls near stoves—but I heard about the others. As a rule the nurses I talked with had had direct experience of children with rat-bites—and they would advise mothers not to feed the littler children in bed, as this might leave scraps to lure the rats that way. A special vermin problem was caused by the tearing down of slums, I learned, for when this happened the rats would move to nearby blocks and infest them heavily. The use of rat poison created another problem: the children might eat it and be sick. The children were also vulnerable to a poison malady called *pica,* which came from picking the plaster out of walls and eating it, to satisfy some craving.

The worst apartment I saw was on 113th Street, three flights up in an old tenement. It had one bedroom, a kitchen, a bathroom, and what might be called a large closet off the kitchen's other side. A Mrs. Rodriguez lived there with seven small children. She paid sixty dollars a month in rent, she said, and drew a hundred and twenty dollars in relief. She also had a husband living elsewhere—whether legally married or not, I cannot say—and he sent her a hundred dollars monthly. The family ate meat three times a week, she said, and when we were there she had some potato cakes and salt codfish on the stove, plus mashed potatoes for the youngest child, an infant. She owned a sewing machine and a small radio, and had a small four-burner gas stove and a double sink in the kitchen. Much of the kitchen's space was taken up with clothes hanging on lines. The bedroom, which was small, had plaster off its walls in spots, one of these being at least a yard wide, with the laths laid bare. Mrs. Rodriguez said the wind came in there, and she had recently had to buy four blankets because of it to keep the children warm. Elsewhere the walls were indescribably dirty—scribbled over, smeared over, and smudged over. The room had one set of double-deck bunk beds, one single bed, one crib, and one little mattress on the floor, the floor itself being uneven and covered with torn, patchy linoleum.

I asked Mrs. Rodriguez if she had any rats or mice.

"Plenty of both," she answered. "But I have a cat. I don't like cats, but it's the only thing to do here."

Then she showed me some of the children's clothes on the lines in the kitchen. They were full of little holes, which she said had been made by rats before the cat had joined the household.

This kind of thing is the lower depths of New York slum life. From that level the Puerto Ricans' circumstances grade upward till they approach the city's middle-class norm. The worst conditions, perhaps, are in old tenements and chopped-up single family houses. Houses with long "railroad" apartments, which occur frequently in and around the

Puerto Rican districts, are comparatively good; they have lots of space through which the many children in a Puerto Rican family can be distributed. The new public housing projects are still better—a great deal better, in fact—but relatively few Puerto Ricans have gotten into them yet.

Special institutions have grown up in New York's Puerto Rican districts—notably food shops, store-front churches, and travel agencies.

The last can be spotted by the sign PASAJES ("passages") on their fronts, and their prevalence in New York shows the tentative quality of this migration—they deal mainly in "thrift"-class plane tickets back to Puerto Rico.

The store-front churches are usually small, spontaneous, community affairs, with a strong evangelical, puritanical, and even holy-roller cast. Most Puerto Ricans are Roman Catholics in theory, but they are not too well integrated or disciplined into the Church on their island. Besides, there has long been an anti-clerical tendency there, and it has been strengthened by nearly six decades of mainland American rule. Many Puerto Ricans who come up are inclined away from the Church to start with, and when they settle into a Puerto Rican neighborhood they find no Church structure dominating its social life, as would be the case at home. So they break off and join one of the Protestant store-front congregations—perhaps one to which relatives or fellow-townsmen of theirs belong already—and this gives them a new focus for their emotions. I have visited only one of these churches, and found it holy roller in the extreme ("Yes, they *do* jump," said the Puerto Rican who took me, in answer to a question I asked as we set out). The place was called the *Verdadera Iglesia de Dios,* or True Church of God, and in it I saw worshippers with rapt expressions and white gauzy veils. Some of them had *maracas,* the rattly gourd musical instruments of the Caribbean, in their hands. The church also had a public-address system, and the preacher wore white linen.

There are said to be many churches on that order in New York now. Of course a vast number of the migrants remain true to the Catholic Church, but as a rule these are absorbed into existing parishes; they don't change the façades on the Puerto Rican streets. Many who *don't* remain true to the Church, besides, continue to use Catholic images—most Puerto Ricans, including Protestants, seem to have a general belief in these.

Besides Christianity, there is said to be a fair amount of spiritualistic—mediumistic—worship among the migrants, and also a bit of voodoo, with voodoo objects being sold in some shops. But Puerto Ricans as a whole practice voodoo much less than do Cubans and Haitians.

The *bodegas,* the Spanish-American food shops, are probably the main landmarks on the Puerto Rican streets. They owe their existence to two things: air transport and the great difference between the island's food habits and our own. "You come to New York from Puerto Rico, and you don't know how the people here eat," a settlement-house psychologist explained to me recently. "Therefore you try to keep your old diet going as much as you can, and the airplane helps you to do so. The factor of technology is very important all through this migration, in fact. It gives the Puerto Ricans benefits that the older immigrants never had, in the days before Buitoni and canned *gefilte* fish. They can preserve their own foods longer and move them here faster."

Plantains are the chief item flown up here from Puerto Rico. They can be seen in bunches, looking like big green bananas, in the rather musty windows of most *bodegas*. Along with them are likely to be assortments of the brown root vegetables (with whitish insides) that Puerto Ricans like, especially the ones called *yuca, yautía,* and *ñame. Yuca* is a long thin root, and I am told it is the same as cassava, the source of tapioca, which grows in tropical Asia too. *Yautía* I have not heard identified with any plant of other regions; it is turnip shaped, with a hairy or fibrous exterior, and looks like certain bulbs. *Ñame* is the taro of the South Pacific and the *yu-t'ou* of China: a longish root that puts up a few yard-high stalks with big heart-shaped leaves—almost like elephant ears, they are, but emerald green in color.

Puerto Ricans will sometimes tell you, mistakenly, that the *ñame* is the yam, for the two words sound much alike. But the yam of course is the sweet potato, something also used by the Puerto Ricans, as is the white potato. In general, Puerto Ricans are great believers in starchy roots that will grow quickly in the soil of their *fincas,* or little island farms; and some of these roots, including the *yuca* and the *ñame,* will virtually grow as you watch. Their compensating defect, to a mainland palate at least, is a sameness verging on tastelessness. Recently I tried several of them, cooked together with plantains and meat, in a stew called *salcocho,* and the chief difference I found in them was one of texture, not taste—their textures ranged almost from the smoothness of soap to the coarseness of mealy apples.

Salcocho is said to be one of the most popular and standard Puerto Rican dishes, and it is often made with tripe and other victuals. *Vianda con bacalao* is another popular dish, made with salt codfish and some of the above roots and vegetables. Puerto Rico is an island and is becoming a center of sport fishing, especially for marlin, yet for some reason its people have not developed their commercial fisheries much. Their great staple fish, without question, is this salt codfish or *bacalao,* which comes out of the Atlantic hundreds of miles to their north. They eat it everywhere on their island, and the New York *bodegas* stock it heavily.

The use of salt codfish derives, presumably, from Spanish cooking, and another thing that derives from it is rice. So far as I have learned, the Puerto Ricans are not much good at making *paella,* the great, and rather dry, Spanish dish of rice and seafood, but they do like the wetter rice stew called *asopao,* with chicken or seafood and vegetables. And the real staple of all Puerto Ricans, rich and poor alike, is rice and beans. In many households two meals a day will be built on this base. If the family is poor, its members will eat the base and not much else; if it is rich, they will eat many other things along with it. In Puerto Rican dwellings in New York, rice and beans are said to be eaten in tremendous volume, and they can always be found in the cheap little restaurants on the city's Puerto Rican streets, along with a few other things like *salcocho* or the dish called *mofongo,* which is made on a base of mashed plantains and pork cracklings.

Rice and beans are available through our normal mainland grocery channels, so they are not among the main attractions of the *bodegas.* Certain rice dishes, though, including a line of *asopaos,* are being canned in Puerto Rico now and shipped up here in that form, and these are prominent on the shelves. Another leading item in the *bodegas* is Puerto Rican coffee—or in some cases Dominican coffee, I am told—which the islanders think, and not without reason, is better than the coffee that we natives drink here.

Thanks to the Puerto Ricans, New York now has about thirty Spanish-language movie houses. A few of the films shown in these come from Spain and Argentina, but the vast majority are Mexican ones, which the Puerto Ricans are said to favor overwhelmingly. They are said to like gangster films and musical dramas, and at times they have liked Westerns a great deal, but are said to be rather off them now.

I have dropped in on Spanish movies in East Harlem and have noted that the girls in the Westerns are spicier than the traditional schoolmarms in our Stateside ones—they may wear black underwear, for instance. The hero in a Mexican Western, again, may kick the villain when the latter is down. The non-Westerns seem to have a good deal more singing, dancing, and vivacity than ours do, not to mention more chandeliers. And I am sure that subtler differences would be found in a more serious study of these Spanish movies. Anyway, the Puerto Ricans flock to them in their ghettos, and a brisk business is done.

The migrants in New York have their choice of three Spanish-language newspapers. One of these, *La Prensa,* antedates the migration by many years; a conservative paper with a sober format, it tries to serve the whole Spanish-speaking community here, which includes a great many businessmen, diplomats, and political exiles from various countries, and it carries much news of Spain and Latin America. A second paper, *El Imparcial,* is a special edition of the San Juan paper of that name, and began New York publication only in 1957; it covers events on the island for the most part. The third, and jazziest, is *El Diario de Nueva York,* a tabloid founded in 1948; it is slanted expressly toward the Puerto Rican migrants, championing them against the police and other city agencies, and plainly seeking to weld them into a political force. Through these papers, tidbits of New York journalistic fare are served up with a Spanish flavor. Maggie and Jiggs become Ramona and Pancho, Blondie becomes Pepita, Mickey Mouse becomes El Raton Miguelito, and in general life around us takes on a new, Iberian aspect.

Of the three papers *El Diario,* being the most consciously popular, is also the most inclined to forsake good Spanish usage for the patois that has grown up among the migrants. I have seen in its pages, for instance, the un-Spanish-looking noun "super," meaning the superintendent of an apartment house or tenement. Supers are awesome figures to New York's Puerto Ricans, and the latter have adopted our name for them intact. A more usual Puerto Rican tendency, though, is to make changes in the English words taken over. There are a great many of these, and the number keeps growing.

Recently an intelligent bilingual Puerto Rican girl, a secretary, told me how the adoptive process functioned in her case. "You work all day speaking English," she said, "and then you go home and speak Spanish for only a few hours in the evening. Or if you watch the TV it is even worse. So you begin to forget your Spanish words because you don't practice them enough. And if you can't think of a Spanish word you use the English word instead, and pretty soon you have a lot of English words in your vocabulary." This girl had recently gone back to Puerto Rico, to visit her family, and she said that while there she had been very careful to keep English words out of her speech, because the home folks would have made fun of her for using them.

Another bilingual Puerto Rican girl in New York has told me that she recently went down to the island, and that the people there hardly understood what she was saying, her speech was so peppered with English.

These two girls, it should be said, are gifted people and have lived in New York a long time. Their English is excellent, and I don't doubt that their Spanish is too, despite what they say about it. In this way they differ from the ordinary migrants, who are often accused of speaking neither tongue well—of "being illiterate in two languages," as it is often put. This complaint usually comes from purists, of Puerto Rican or other Hispanic background, and I don't know how seriously it should be taken. No doubt the same thing has been said of other migrants since the dawn of history. But there it is.

Many New York Puerto Ricans say "guachiman" for "watchman," which is purely a transposition from English. They say "rufo" for "roof," instead of the proper Spanish word "techo." They speak of "el moppa" and "el estore" for "the mop" and "the store." Among the words that they change less than this, merely putting a Spanish article on them, are "el window," "el movie," and "el subway."

The gender nearly always becomes masculine, for some reason, when nouns are taken over this way, but occasionally a feminine one crops up: "la marqueta," for instance, is the patois word for our institution of "the supermarket"; there is a perfectly good Spanish word "el mercado" for "the market," but the Puerto Ricans do not use it.

English verbs are said to be much less frequent than English nouns in the patois, but some do exist there; among them are "parquear," for "park" a car, and "moppear," for "mop" a floor. In some special fields the borrowing of English words is done still more crudely. In labor-union literature, for instance, words like "steward," "open shop," and "closed shop" are printed just that way in Spanish texts, without any attempt at translating.

Even aside from the English in their vocabularies, the

Puerto Ricans speak a brand of Spanish that alarms many purists from the old country and from parts of South America. "They speak very fast and cut their words off at the ends," a Chilean purist recently lamented in my presence. "And then they change the word order around, perhaps because of English influence. Instead of 'Que escribe usted?' ('What are you writing?') which of course is correct, they shift the order to 'Que usted escribe?' Or for 'Adonde va usted?' ('Where are you going'?) they say, 'Adonde usted va?' No they don't, either. They say 'Adonde tu va?' because they use the familiar 'tu' instead of the formal 'usted,' as they should. With us this is perfectly terrible, you know. It is like an insult." And the Chilean shook his head and sighed.

Music is a Puerto Rican import that transplants especially well to the mainland. The Puerto Ricans are a dancing people. They have to have music wherever they go, and they arrange to get it in this strange land. Much of it comes to them through their radios, for several New York stations now broadcast Spanish programs. Much also comes out of the juke-boxes in the bars and restaurants they frequent.

But live music is best, of course, and for this reason there are many Puerto Rican dance halls in New York, each functioning a few nights a week. They range from little dives to really big establishments like the Tropicana Club in the Bronx and the Caborrojeño in Washington Heights; but the most central and city-wide, perhaps, is the Palladium at Broadway and 53rd Street. It is not the most typical, to be sure, as it is rather expensive, has a good deal of jazz mixed with its music, and is patronized by many people who are not Puerto Ricans. Yet it is probably the handiest place for ordinary New Yorkers to touch the Puerto Rican world, and it is so located that Puerto Ricans themselves can come to it, by subway, from any part of the city if so inclined—it is not identified with any one ghetto.

The Palladium is upstairs in a two-story building. It has a good layout of bar, cloakrooms, and other facilities, and over the dance-floor itself hangs a circular canopy—a sort of tentlike updrawn rosette, about fifty feet in diameter—made of a sage-green material, perhaps nylon. On the far side of the floor, as you come in, is the orchestra's dais, the wall behind it carrying the legends "MERENGUE," "CHA-CHA-CHA," and "CARIBBEAN PALLADIUM: THE HOME OF THE MAMBO."

When I have visited the Palladium its orchestra has usually had eleven pieces, including much brass. It has played a fair amount of jazz, as noted above—at times even when playing Latin music, it has let the melody die out, and then the drums have seemed to keep on with more of a jazz than a Latin rhythm to them. But at other times the Latin element has been supreme. Then the band-leader has had a pair of *maracas* in his hands, and the tunes have been *merengues* and *cha-cha-chas*.

Most of the dancers have always been Puerto Rican—some of the men zoot-suited, some of the men and some of the women chewing gum. Usually they have been young, but one evening I remember a dark, middle-aged, heavyish Puerto Rican couple who had come out to enjoy themselves in their national pastime and were doing so with grace and sentiment, rather as one might expect Darby and Joan to do.

In general I have felt that the Palladium has more gaiety and good spirit than the run of New York night clubs, and my partner on excursions there has agreed. The Puerto Ricans dominate the place, but there is usually a sprinkling of mainland whites and a goodly number of mainland Negroes. The Puerto Ricans, and those who can keep up with them, dance the *merengue* with liquid hips, moving around fast and sometimes passing their partners under their arms. Sometimes there is a *merengue* contest, staged with dramatic spotlighting, and several couples take part in it. Each couple has only an instant to show their stuff. Then the master of ceremonies holds a handkerchief over their heads; the crowd votes by clapping or booing; and the next couple comes on lickety-split. Group lessons in the *merengue* and *cha-cha-cha* are also given at the Palladium, on Wednesday nights, when hundreds of customers go out on the floor to stamp their feet in ghostly unison, without music.

The origins of Caribbean music are but dimly understood. *Maracas* are said to have existed in the region before Columbus got there, and some experts think they originated in Puerto Rico itself among the aboriginal Indians, the Borinqueños. Another ancient Puerto Rican instrument is the *güiro,* a hollow gourd that is sounded by rubbing a file-like stick against its side.

The Spanish music that crossed the Atlantic has been affected by the primitive qualities of these instruments, and also by the African slave influx to the Caribbean. As time passed, different dances have developed on the different islands, and later have moved about between them. It is generally agreed that the *merengue* began long, long ago in the present Dominican Republic; but now it is the Puerto Rican's favorite dance; and it has started to take hold on the mainland largely through Puerto Rican sponsorship. The *cha-cha-cha* probably began in Cuba; but it too is popular in Puerto Rico; and it too is permeating much of the whole non-Communist world, again with Puerto Rican help. Other dances of the Puerto Ricans include the *paso doble,* a stately one said to have come down from Spanish bullfight music, and the *bolero,* a sort of foxtrot said to be danced all through the Spanish New World. There are song-forms, too, and song-and-dance combinations that the Puerto Ricans fancy; these include *aguinaldos,* which are like Christmas carols, and *plenas,* which are said to be very prevalent in the island's country districts and which tell improvised current legends, much as do calypso songs.

Calypso singing, incidentally, belongs to the Caribbean, but not to the Spanish tradition that graces Puerto Rico. The same is true of steel-band music. The Caribbean islands have been ruled by various Western countries, and their musical culture varies accordingly, with Cuba, the Dominican Republic, and Puerto Rico being the chief bearers of the Spanish style.

The Spanish Caribbean in turn has its relationships, musically, with other parts of New Spain, in Central and South America. From those other parts have come the *mambo* and the *conga,* which have little to do with Puerto Rico except by recent adoption. The *tango,* the oldest Spanish form popular with us mainlanders, comes from certain of those other parts too, and from Spain itself. The *rumba* is our second-oldest Spanish form (dating back here to the early 1930s), and it comes from Cuba, again with little or no Puerto Rican impetus. But nowadays it can be said that Puerto Rico is the main bearer of Spanish music toward our shores, especially of the *merengue* and the *cha-cha-cha.* These are affecting vast parts of humanity, and the Puerto Rican influx to New York has much to do with it.

I have watched the *merengue* danced a good deal, in both New York and Puerto Rico, and sometimes in the company of experts. Among its characteristics is a very brassy timbre in the orchestra. One seven-piece orchestra that I heard playing in Puerto Rico had two horns and two saxophones in it (the other instruments being drums, a piano, and a pair of *maracas* alternating with a *güiro*). Whenever a *merengue* was played, the music positively blared and flared out, filling the room with a sunny, metallic warmth. The dancers used a lot of supple, sideways hip motion. This was so extreme, and so fast, that it seemed to distort the human frame and its functions.

"The *merengue* is sometimes called the dance with the limp," a companion told me. "Actually, the hip motion is strictly a result of what you do with your feet, and that is why so many mainlanders make fools of themselves when they try it. In general, Latin American dances are not a question of knowing a certain step, but of hearing the beat and moving to it. If you can hear the beat and move to it you are doing the dance. Diagramming it, in the manner of a New York dancing teacher, just makes it rigid and louses it up. The Puerto Ricans themselves would never do that because they are born with a sense of rhythm."

In the old Puerto Rican culture Three Kings Day—or Twelfth-Night or Epiphany—is a greater celebration than Christmas, and recently on that day I went to a children's party on Manhattan's Upper West Side, in a YMCA building. The party was supposed to begin at 2:30, but it got going rather late, as Puerto Rican festivities often do. After three o'clock though, there were two or three dozen children on hand—all bundled up, for it was cold and we were sitting in a chilly basketball court—and the Puerto Rican women who were running the affair began playing some Christmas carols on the phonograph. These were on topics like Good King Wenceslas, and I felt they didn't mean much to the children. Later the women began singing them some *aguinaldos* and telling them about Three Kings Day, but this didn't seem to mean much to them either—perhaps, I imagined, the children had lost touch with the old traditions in New York. After the *aguinaldos* were finished, a little Puerto Rican girl played some carols on an accordion, and she did it well.

But the party didn't really warm up till someone put a *merengue* record on the phonograph and a girl of seven or eight went out and danced to it solo. She wore a blue sweater, a black figured skirt, black pumps, and pink socks. She had much freer hip action than one would expect in any mainland girl of that age, and she danced with a serious, businesslike air. Later, another little girl did a *cha-cha-cha*, which involved lots of kicking and footwork, and she too was very serious and proficient. Soon other children, some of them just toddlers, came out on the floor or were pushed there by their parents, and for a while the party turned into a lively, if midget, Latin dance festival, with the music resonant in the wooden hall. And during that phase it really *was* a party, too.

In that same season I went to another Three Kings Day festival, at a settlement house, and it turned out much the same. This time the management, which was not Puerto Rican, had arranged for a magician, a pageant, and other orthodox entertainments, but the children themselves had arranged for two girls of their number to do Latin dances on the stage. These girls were more mature than those at the other party, and they wore abbreviated costumes and danced with a suppleness almost beyond belief. A few of the settlement-house people were shocked by it, I sensed, but the children themselves weren't. To them it was absolutely natural.

Some time later a Puerto Rican friend was discoursing to me on New York customs. "Our folks can't understand your parties," he said, "because people just seem to sit around and talk—they sit and drink and look at each other. With us a party isn't a party without a dance." He sighed. "We think folks here just don't know how to enjoy themselves," he said. And I am sure he spoke truly for his people.

II *Down on the Island*

Puerto Rico is a green island amid deep blue water. To the north the water is called the Atlantic Ocean, to the south it is the Caribbean Sea; Puerto Rico is a link in the chain of islands, the Antilles, that divides these two. The chain's west end is Cuba, south of Florida; then come Jamaica and the island of Hispaniola, shared by Haiti and the Dominican Republic; then Puerto Rico; and after that the Antilles curve southward through the Leeward and Windward Islands till they end at Trinidad, off the Venezuelan coast.

Puerto Rico's prevailing winds are from the Atlantic, and its north shore gets most of the rainfall. A spine of mountains follows its long axis, which runs for a hundred miles, from west to east; on their south side, toward the Caribbean, the vegetation has a tawny strain from drought, but on the north it is a deep moist tropical green. In the jungles on that side grow big trees, creepers, and giant ferns, and in the settled places hibiscus, oleanders, bougainvillea, and poinsettias tall as lilacs—everywhere pink, red, mauve, and orange blooms are seen against the green background. It is always balmy in Puerto Rico—never cold, seldom very hot—and one can live right out in nature all the time.

From our Western view Puerto Rico was discovered in 1493, by Christopher Columbus on his second voyage. One of his companions then was Juan Ponce de León, who later returned to colonize Puerto Rico, become its first governor, and subdue the Indians there—the Borqueños. Ponce de León is known to American schoolboys as an old man who went to Florida in search of the fountain of youth, but the ludicrous picture this suggests is unfair. A statue of Ponce de León, in greenish-bronze and a bit smaller than life, stands in a square of San Juan, the Puerto Rican capital. He wears a plumed hat, sword, and high boots, and looks every inch the strong *conquistador*. Inscriptions round the statue's pedestal say, among other things, that he finished his conquest of Puerto Rico in 1511, that he later discovered Florida, and that he was mortally wounded there [by Indians] in 1521, dying soon afterward in Cuba. He was undoubtedly a leading creator of the Spanish New World and an important figure in American history—today Puerto Ricans sometime point out, jokingly, that Ponce de León was the first migrant from their island to our continent.

In early Spanish days the island of Puerto Rico was called San Juan Baptista, or St. John the Baptist, and its capital was called Puerto Rico, or Rich Port; since then the two names have simply been transposed. The island and the city were both important in the old strategy of the Spanish Main, for they helped to guard the passage through which convoys of Spanish galleons entered the Caribbean on their way to pick up Mexican, Peruvian, and Philippine riches at Vera Cruz and at Portobelo on the Isthmus. These convoys were deemed fair prey by Spain's enemies, and in the campaigns against them San Juan's defenses were attacked many times, by the British and the Dutch, in the sixteenth, seventeenth, and eighteenth centuries. One British attack was led by Sir Francis Drake, who, during it, had his stool shot out from under him while at supper on his flagship.

In the nineteenth century these European quarrels calmed down, as far as the New World was concerned, but other troubles began. Spain's hold on her empire weakened, and most of her American colonies split off and declared their independence. Then finally, in 1898, the Spanish-American War broke out—its main cause being the Cuban independence struggle—and in the course of it Puerto Rico became a United States possession, though it was not especially prized as such, or even much thought about. It was officially known, right up into the 1930s, as "Porto" Rico, a spelling that is illiterate by the rules of Spanish.

Most Americans who have studied the matter feel that Washington neglected Puerto Rico in the first three or four decades of our rule there—even till 1941, when Rexford Tugwell was made the island's governor. One such student is Henry L. McCarthy, New York's Commissioner of Welfare, who knows the Puerto Ricans well. "We neglected Puerto Rico right across the board," McCarthy said recently, "—in health, education, public works, everything. It wasn't till Tugwell went there that we began living up to our responsibilities. Tugwell did a lot for public health and other social services, and since his time we have treated the island more as it deserved."

For all the official neglect, though, certain non-governmental forces from our mainland went to work on Puerto Rico, changing things there. American business went in and began selling American goods by American methods—today one hears that Puerto Ricans know much more about installment buying than do other Latin Americans. They have also acquired a hunger for the gadgets money can buy, and cash now plays a part in their lives undreamt of in the nineteenth century. Many Protestant missionaries also went to Puerto Rico from the mainland after 1898, penetrating and disturbing what had previously been a quiet domain of the Catholic Church.

"The new missionaries bustled about," a sociologist who has been studying Puerto Rico said the other day, "and they

began presenting Christianity to the island as a religion of
works—linked with uplift, change, ambition, and all that—
rather than a religion of the *status quo,* as Spanish Catholi-
cism had been. They founded schools, hospitals, and farm-
improvement stations. They taught a belief in material
progress. They encouraged Puerto Ricans to join the clergy,
which the Spanish Catholic Church had never done, fearing
that an anti-colonial leadership might develop that way. In
short, the new missionaries implanted the so-called Protestant ethic on the island, and this led, inevitably, to things
like a new middle class, a new money economy, and bigger
commercial cities."

The money economy was further encouraged by United
States investments, especially in the sugar plantations and
refineries. In the old days sugar had been a patriarchal enterprise of landed families, with oxcarts, small boiling-
plants, and workers attached to the soil. Now it became
mechanized, with huge mills owned by corporations, and
with rootless workers dependent on cash wages, who made
up a rural proletariat. Then some of these drifted to the
cities, and made up an urban proletariat too. In some
respects, that is, Puerto Rico was quickly modernized.

One result was a big climb in the population, owing
mainly to a fall in the death rate, which came in turn from
modern medicine brought in through the new hospitals.
Between 1900 and 1950 the population more than doubled
—from less than a million to well over two million—and
Puerto Rico became one of the world's most uncomfortably
crowded places. In the 1930s the island was sometimes described as a desperate poor-house, with a calamitous future
ahead.

Actually this future has not materialized, because of two
developments—the great Puerto Rican migration to New

York and the island's new-deal administration under Luis Muñoz Marín, which has done wonders in things like education, public housing, and economic development, the last of which, in the "Operation Bootstrap" program, is transforming much of the island's life.

In the spring of 1957 I visited Puerto Rico in hopes of learning more about the migrants in New York. The strongest impression I got, on the whole, was an aesthetic one—of how well the Puerto Ricans fitted into their own landscape. In New York they often have a dingy look, in my experience, but this isn't true on their island. They wear brighter colors there, and cotton clothes the year round, which they wash often. They look absolutely natural against their green background—standing in the mottled shade, say, of some casuarina trees, with the soft breeze ruffling their hair.

In the evening they look natural, too, as they stroll in San Juan or some other town. In New York they crowd out on the sidewalks on warm evenings, but this is not the same thing. In Puerto Rico they have plazas, or squares, to crowd into, with green trees and pleasant backdrops of white buildings (San Juan's plazas also have public TV sets in them now, thanks to the present municipal government). The people frequent the plazas in the warm night, gossiping or playing games, and they look as if they belonged there. Often in San Juan I saw old men sitting at tables on the curbstones, playing dominoes. And I remember a taxi-driver who sat by his vehicle on a little camp chair of slatted wood. I asked him to take me somewhere, and before doing so he merely folded the chair and put it on the front seat beside him. All Puerto Ricans seem practiced at taking the fresh air, and ready to do so when they can.

Twice in the evening I went to a night-club in San Juan,

which had good Latin American music. It was a sprawling frame structure, reminiscent of certain ones in our seaside resorts or amusements parks, of a few decades back. It was beside a lagoon, on piles or stilts, and the festivities took place in what amounted to the second story. The dance-floor was of plain wood, and the walls and ceilings were of wood painted simply in light blue and light green, colors that are popular everywhere in the tropics. The chairs and tables were very plain and cool looking. All around the place were horizontal windows open to the outer world—to the lagoon and the neighboring rooftops—and one night when I was there a full moon shone on this scene, giving it an enchantment that simply can't be duplicated in New York, where the Puerto Rican hot-spots are tightly closed against the elements.

Another day, in the afternoon, when I was passing the Sixto Escobar Stadium, a big establishment near my hotel, I heard a great uproar inside it. I went to an entrance gate, found a woman there, and asked her (in English) what was going on.

"Just a field day for the children," she said.

I asked if the public was admitted, and she said no, but that I could come in anyway, though I wouldn't be allowed to pay. I entered and took my place in the grandstand, which was about three-quarters full of school-children, mainly teen-agers. A big stage had been built over home plate and part of the infield, and when I arrived a number of girls were dancing on this to some Latin rhythm. They wore bright flaring skirts and white blouses with lacy or frilly collars, and they danced well in a sort of chorus formation. They finished, and the athletic events began, on a track round the ball field.

There were lots of races and jumping contests between

children of various sizes, and they were run off with dis-
patch, sometimes two events being staged simultaneously
in different places. In the boys' events those who finished
first, second, and third were taken to a small platform where
stood three girls dressed in white, and they would lean
forward to pin insignia on the winners and kiss them as
they did so.

The crowd in the stadium numbered a few thousand
children, and they were well behaved, clean, and enthusias-
tic. Their composition seemed what one would expect in a
crowd of young New York Puerto Ricans—their distribution
through the color range seemed the same, for one thing—
and I couldn't help remarking that in New York many of
them might be thought, on the law of averages, to be
juvenile delinquents. But here they seemed innocent-look-
ing, and their complexions were fresh and blooming, if
sometimes moist in the heat.

After a while a boy started to beat a drum in the grandstand behind me, with very stirring rhythm, and a number
of the children gathered there and shuffled or danced. Elsewhere children began to cheer rhythmically, too. I left soon
afterward. Many in the crowd, I felt, were getting rather
excited, but it seemed a harmless mood that could lead to
no trouble.

During my visit I walked often in old San Juan, which
may well be the most picturesque town on United States
soil. It is small, and consists mainly of stucco buildings
ranged along narrow cobbled streets. Many of the buildings
are painted in water-ice colors, and some are very old; often
a passageway will lead back, from the main door in a façade,
to a patio in the rear, round which small apartments will
have their entrances in ancient privacy. The cobbles in the

streets are brick shaped, and of a blue porous stone said to be imported from Spain; at midday they reflect the blue sky with intensity.

The streets are hilly. Through their north ends one sometimes sees the blue Atlantic, and through their south ends one usually sees San Juan Bay, with green mountains beyond it. The streets are so narrow that only one-way traffic is possible in them, and even this must crawl. The sidewalks are just wide enough for one person to walk in comfort. Here and there they have parking-meters on them, but these are placed on the inside, next to the buildings—if placed on the curbs, presumably, they would be too much in the way in those close quarters.

San Juan has two magnificent old Spanish forts, looking on the ocean and the bay, and an old white palace for the governor, surrounded by tropical foliage. It is a city that stubbornly resists modern times—and mainly, it seems, by being on such a small scale. Our big new American cars are hopelessly cramped there, and the shops are nearly all tiny, with small bright merchandise displayed in their windows in a straightforward, old-fashioned way. One can hardly imagine streamlining San Juan without tearing it down and starting again.

The twentieth century has expressed itself less in the city proper than in a suburb, Santurce, which has been built almost entirely since 1898. This has much in common with Los Angeles, or with cities in Florida, or even with the newest suburbs of the big Asian cities—it has wide streets, that is, heavy traffic, white or near-white stucco buildings—some of them quite tall—and a welter of modern signs, modern shop-windows, and other visual clamor of the advertising age.

"Santurce is a tropical suburb of New York," one Puerto

Rican told me, and this seems a fair statement. The New York influence, one might say, leap-frogged the old city and landed on Santurce instead.

Still farther inland, however, in still newer suburbs—and out into the country beside the big new roads—a further degree of modernization is in progress, for the island is in a fever of construction through Operation Bootstrap. If you drive westward from San Juan and Santurce, on the north coast highway, you will constantly find yourself being loomed over by great noisy trailer-trucks; and you will pass tracts of land that are being bulldozed and generally slapped around in preparation for new factories. As you drive along you come to feel that no other part of the earth's surface can be undergoing such great change now.

But then again, beyond the suburbs and beyond the roadside fringe, the old tropical landscape takes over once more, with its greenness. On the island's north side one sees rolling greenness, pure and simple, with what appear to be miscellaneous farms. In the center—in the mountains—the scene is more jungley, and wilder, and the settlements are often isolated. Then on the south side there is a heavy concentration on sugar, with vast expanses—often irrigated—of the rich green cane. When I was there last spring it was the middle of the *zafra,* or sugar-harvest, and trucks piled high with cane were frequent on the southern roads. Men were out in the fields cutting the crop. And here and there the refineries, like big factories, were going full blast, with dark smoke pouring from their chimneys.

The commonest works of man in many Puerto Rican landscapes are small boxlike wooden houses, often set on stilts and often painted in bright colors—usually blue or green, for coolness, but sometimes red or yellow. A house may have a patch of root-vegetables by it, or bananas or plantains—small trees, these are, with huge blue-green fringed leaves.

Some houses are very small—a single room will do, if need be, for a family of half a dozen, because it is supplemented by the great outdoors; I have even heard of Puerto Rican households that put their beds outside in the daytime, to make more room, and take them in again at night.

Some houses have remarkably few possessions in them. Recently an exhaustive survey of living standards was made, by sociologists, in Puerto Rico, and they found that many poor rural families had no more than seven pieces of furniture in their homes, a typical list of which included a bench, a table, a chest, a bed, a hammock, a cot, and a shelf. The same survey found that poor families sometimes slept five, ten, or even more to a room; and three, four, or five to a double bed. They made up for these shortages by spending much of their time out of doors, where they also threw their garbage away, and generally yielded nature's surplus back to her. They washed their clothes in a nearby stream and relied on the sun to tell time—though time was really not of great moment to them. Such families were, and still are, living what can be called a primitive, idyllic life, though it is less primitive than that still lived in parts of Cuba and Haiti, where palmthatched huts are said to be the rule. In Puerto Rico one sees very little thatch.

The simple life is being abandoned rapidly in Puerto Rico now, because many people are moving to the towns and the standards throughout the island are being modernized. New stucco or cement dwellings can be seen everywhere, and public-housing projects galore can be seen in the towns —San Juan, with its suburbs, is sometimes called the world's best-endowed city now, in regard to public housing, a distinction it has won with considerable help from Washington.

Even so, the basic Puerto Rican unit of shelter still seems —to a casual observer—to be the wooden-box house, which proliferates in town and country alike. Around San Juan it proliferates in stilted shantytowns, mainly on mudflats by the bay and the lagoons. The best-known of these, El Fanguito ("The Little Mud"), was originally built entirely over tidewater, I have been told, but since then a substantial, if rather jagged, layer of crushed stone has been laid underneath it to make solid ground. The little houses rise from this in their cool blues and greens. Sometimes they are fenced in with bits of corrugated iron; often they have skinny dogs round them, barking; and often, too, the ground near them is littered with refuse, though the government is waging an intense clean-up drive. Nearly always, too, the houses are infested with mosquitoes after dark.

A more pleasant shantytown is the one called La Perla ("The Pearl"), which clings to a steep, almost clifflike hillside between old San Juan and the ocean. I went down to the bottom of this one day at low tide. There were green mossy rocks there, with waves breaking on them, and inside them a narrow beach of brown sand. Rocks and sand were bedecked with innumerable rounded, bright-colored bits of glass, which I assumed came from bottles broken long ago and ground interminably by the surf. La Perla rose in tiers above me on the slope; I could make out five nearly distinct levels, not to mention half-levels and other irregularities. The shanties were in the hundreds or thousands. Some were of weathered frame, some were covered with black or green tarpaper, and others were painted: a few in egg-yolk yellow, more in blues, and still more in various greens—I could distinguish a half dozen shades of this last.

Some shanties seemed really flimsy, some substantial. A few had TV antennas coming out of their roofs. I began walking up through the tiers, and I found that many shanties rested on old foundations, like shelves, of concrete or masonry, which I guessed must have been there a long time. Paths struggled upward, through the tiers, on steps. Sometimes they ducked round the shanties, sometimes they disappeared inside them. I met with many open doorways; through some I saw little but bare walls and floor, through others good solid furniture—a set of cane-bottom chairs and a sofa, for example.

The children I saw were neat and relatively well dressed, and often they were playing games, perhaps marbles. Here and there old men sat on their stoops, or were gathered at tiny shack cafés, half out of doors. They were smoking and taking it easy, and they didn't seem to mind my intrusion. I felt a friendly atmosphere round the whole place, indeed, and also much beauty. Out in the distance lay the azure sea. Down on the shore the white spray leapt high off the rocks, and above it the cool breeze flooded in through the airy shacks. La Perla was a slum all right, but it almost seemed a paradise of slums.

Another thing on which I got impressions, if not very sharp ones, was the racial and class division among Puerto Ricans, a matter that affects their adjustment to New York considerably. A National Park Service guide, who took me through San Juan's main old fort one day, remarked in passing that Negroes made up 22 per cent of the island's population, and I suppose that is as good a figure as any—in this question much depends, inevitably, on where one draws the line. The Negro stock is descended from African slaves brought in by the Spanish to replace the native Indian population, which they had largely killed, or driven into hiding or exile, by their stiff system of forced labor. Eventually the slaves were freed, and they have intermarried with other Puerto Ricans, producing the variously mixed types that can be seen now in the Puerto Rican sections of New York, among other places.

Before going to Puerto Rico I had heard conflicting reports on the state of color discrimination there, and as I went about San Juan I tried to note the prevalence of one shade or another in the crowds I saw. I found that in El Fanguito, the shantytown, there was a high proportion of dark faces. On the campus of the University of Puerto Rico, on the other hand—which is a training-ground for the wealthier families—I found a low proportion of them. On Sundays at the Caribe Hilton Hotel, again, I saw dozens of Puerto Ricans taking their ease alongside the mainland tourists, but none of these was dark. None of the high government officials I met was dark, either, and I believe this is the rule or tendency, though it has many exceptions.

Finally, on some occasions I saw groups, predominantly dark, that seemed to be set apart from the general populace and to be linked together by family or social ties. The most notable of these was at a funeral in San Juan. The funeral party came out of an old church late one afternoon, as I was walking by it. There was an auto to carry the flowers, but the coffin itself was carried by pallbearers, who walked solemnly, surrounded by a few dozen mourners, on the blue cobbles in the afternoon shadows. Three-quarters of the people in that crowd were dark, as if the funeral were of interest mainly to a special community that was inside the larger populace, but not quite of it.

From these sights, and from conversations, I gathered that the Negroes were a people somewhat apart in Puerto

Rico, but less drastically so than on our mainland. Man for man, they seemed at an economic, or class, disadvantage compared to whites, as witness their frequency in El Fanguito and their rarity at the University and in the high ranks of government. This disadvantage presumably went far back in history, too, as it is not the kind of thing that is created overnight.

One sometimes hears that there was no race prejudice in Puerto Rico before 1898, and that our mainland example has introduced it since then. Yet this can hardly be true unless one takes "prejudice" in a sense implying repugnance or condemnation—a putting of the Negroes quite beyond the pale, that is. I had the feeling that the absence of dark Puerto Ricans at the Caribe Hilton was tinged with this sort of prejudice.

Their rarity in other places seemed a different matter, though, and was not complete. Some did attend the University, I learned, and some did get into the high ranks of government. Some were even linked by marriage to certain leading families. That these privileged ones were only a small minority, I gathered, could be laid mainly to the fact that Negroes were, by origin, a part of the laboring class, and that members of that class seldom rose much in the old Puerto Rican society, which was Spanish-colonial and stratified. "On our United States mainland we have a lot of social mobility," one expert on Puerto Rico explained to me. "People there go from rags to riches all the time. But the Negroes are largely segregated outside this process. In traditional Puerto Rico, on the other hand, there has been little social mobility. The masses have been illiterate and have been expected to stay underneath. And the Negroes, by and large, have been part of that submerged class."

Some Puerto Ricans I have met have been critical of our

race prejudice, but have not—or so it has seemed to me—taken corresponding note of their own class prejudice, which in its way seems almost as exclusive—and which still exists, though it is weakening under mainland influence. At the top of Puerto Rican society, one usually hears, are a few hundred families of almost unmixed European ancestry, which in the old days were closely identified with Spain and are now identified, at least partly, with the United States mainland and mainland business. Between these families and the masses there used to be only a small number of white-collar clerical workers—in the government, Church, and business—though now a fast-growing middle class is moving into that area. The masses themselves were—and still are, to some degree—like the unlettered peasantry in any non-modern country: an uncounted human sea on which the aristocracy can float.

"The masses of our people are rootless and without hope," an extra-candid Puerto Rican in New York has told me. "They have no sense of identification and no sense of the future. And those in our middle class have a defensive attitude toward them. They shut poverty out of their minds, and they don't recognize the true facts about the poor. So they don't understand them, and you get ingrained class or caste prejudices." This man was perhaps exaggerating—and anyway the Puerto Rican class lines seem to be fast dissolving—but I felt that his words, even so, must have had some basis in fact.

From mainlanders in Puerto Rico I heard many favorable comments on the islanders' temperament—strikingly different, these were, from the things most New Yorkers say about them. Puerto Ricans are repeatedly described by the mainlanders among them as happy, friendly, and courteous.

Their kindness to children is often mentioned, and indeed this trait is plain to the eye of a visitor—children are allowed to do almost anything in Puerto Rico, one feels after being there awhile.

In general Puerto Ricans seem not to take life, or their own institutions, too seriously, and this goes for the Church among other things. "Puerto Rico is a Catholic country where the women practice and the men abstain," one mainlander friend told me in San Juan. "Often on Sundays I have seen a man and wife drive up to church in a car, and seen the man let the wife out and drive away again."

This friend told me that one of the Church's main functions in Puerto Rico was to supply festivals that the children could enjoy. For the sake of the children, he added, the Puerto Ricans had recently been expanding their celebration of Christmas. In their old culture Three Kings Day, or the Epiphany, had been their main winter festival, and they had customarily given their children presents then. But since the United States has taken Puerto Rico over, our mainland custom of Christmas, with its potentiality for still more presents, has gradually become known there, and now the Puerto Ricans are celebrating both days—though they are only twelve nights apart—and are giving presents on both of them, too.

The Puerto Ricans' love of music also makes itself apparent on the island. Music stores seem inordinately frequent in cities like San Juan, and every little bar in Puerto Rico—there are a great many of these, often painted in tropical blue or green—seems to have a huge juke-box standing in it like a shrine, with its weirdly colored lights. Most of the records in the juke-boxes are *merengues*, *cha-cha-chas* and other Latin American dances, but there are usually a few rock-and-roll pieces too—rock-and-roll being, apparently, an almost universal style these days. (Most Puerto Ricans, incidentally, drink rum or beer; innumerable brands of the former are made on the island, and three brands of the latter, too, all of them palatable. The islanders apparently seldom drink to excess, though occasionally one meets a staggerer, of an evening, in the streets of San Juan.)

One entrancing musical sight I saw was at El Morro, the main old Spanish fort in San Juan. I was going through there on a guided tour, and at one point, next to a thick and ancient wall of masonry, we came upon a United States Army band in rehearsal. It was of mixed Puerto Rican and mainland personnel, all sitting there in fatigue uniforms complete with hash-marks—looking very orthodox, that is, and led by an orthodox-looking warrant-officer. The instruments looked orthodox too—mainly of brass, and mainly unchanged since Sousa's day—except that one player had in his hands a pair of *maracas,* or Puerto Rican gourd rattles. And the tune they all were practicing was a lively *mambo.* They sat there playing the *mambo* in the sunshine, and for all their khaki, and all their brass horns, they seemed to belong to a different, non-GI world as we listened to them. The Puerto Rican influence can, it seems, be most pervasive.

Why Puerto Ricans leave home is a question one gets many answers to. A couple of these are definite and incontrovertible: Puerto Ricans leave home because there are too many of them there, and because they can earn more money in New York or its hinterland. Even despite the migration to our mainland, 15 per cent of the Puerto Rican labor force is said to be unemployed now, and another 15 per cent employed but partially; able-bodied men with any ambition naturally abhor that situation. As for the pay difference, one often hears that Puerto Ricans can earn twice as much in New York as on their island, and that living costs in the two places differ little except for the item of fuel and warm clothes in the New York winter. This is probably an exaggeration, yet by and large more pay *can* be made in New York (in good times)—and more can be saved, too, or spent on TV sets or washing machines.

Studies have shown that the volume of Puerto Rican migration varies directly with the volume of jobs available in New York, and has for a long time. The migration was heavy right after VJ-Day, and then slackened off in the late 'forties, but it boomed again after the Korean War broke out in 1950, bringing full employment to the United States as a whole. Puerto Rican officials maintain that the migration can be used as an index of our mainland economy, so closely are the two linked.

"We know exactly when there's to be a recession on the mainland," one such official remarked to me. "We have only to watch the Puerto Ricans coming back here. They are the last to be hired and the first to be fired, and if a slump is coming they know it right away."

Psychologically, the Puerto Rican migration of the past decade seems to have its origin in a restlessness brought on by the Second World War. This condition has been more or less global. Since the war stirred things up country people— often refugees—have been piling into big cities all around the world—such as Rome, Bombay, Calcutta, Shanghai, and Los Angeles—and have tended to stay in them, often in miserable shantytowns, even though they haven't been able to make a real living. There has been a general flight away from Nature and the primitive. Even American Indians who served in the War have been loath to go back to their reservations.

In Puerto Rico the fever has had its special characteristics. For one thing, the movement to the city has often been in two stages—first to San Juan, or to another Puerto Rican town like Ponce or Mayagüez, and secondly to New York. And then in Puerto Rico the wartime disturbance itself took a special form. The island was virtually blockaded, over a long period, by Hitler's submarines, and there was a great shortage of things to buy. Meanwhile lots of Puerto Rican youth were drafted, and taken around by Uncle Sam to see the world and its possibilities; and concurrently we set up garrisons and establishments on the island, which spent money in a way unprecedented there. Puerto Rico became a key spot in the air defense of the Panama Canal; and a big naval base, Roosevelt Roads, was built on the island's east end for the British fleet if it had to run from home.

All these things were unsettling to Puerto Rican life, and then the war's end brought another drastic change: the old sea transport to the mainland was not restored—for passengers anyway—but was replaced by airlines, which brought New York much closer.

Some time ago a knowledgeable Puerto Rican in New York told me why he thought the migration had begun. "Of course it began because of overcrowding in Puerto Rico," he said, "and because of the island's inability to take care of the people. We really have an American standard of living there, you see. Even in the 'thirties many of the basic commodities were imported from the mainland. The people began to yearn first for a radio, then for an automobile, and eventually for a TV set. After the war they began seeing new types of food, even—frozen food and so forth. Their desires were aroused; cash became more and more important to them, and New York was the place to get it. There were other reasons too. Some people thought they could better the lot of their children by coming here, even if they couldn't better their own. The government provides a university and schools in Puerto Rico, it is true, but they are not so many as here. There are other social benefits in New York too. It's not just relief that I mean—it's most unfair to say that Puerto Ricans come here for relief. But you have good unions in New York. You have health benefits. You have old-age pensions. You have social security. These things are at higher figures here because the wages are higher, and Puerto Ricans began to learn about it.

"Another thing that helped was letters back. A good job in Puerto Rico would pay eighteen, twenty, twenty-two dollars a week. But in New York even a newcomer would get thirty-five or forty dollars a week, and the expense wouldn't be greater, outside of winter. So when people in the island heard this they thought they should move. They aren't at all dumb about figuring things, you know."

Letters back to Puerto Rico are part of the so-called family intelligence service, whose results are impressive. The new tendency in Puerto Rico is for the family to become small in concept, even boiling down to just parents and their immediate children, after the mainland pattern. But the old customs, under which the family is thought of as extensive, are still much in force, and this big family makes a fine vehicle for the intelligence service to work through. The Migrant Division of the Puerto Rican Department of Labor's New York office says that a few years ago it placed thirty-six Puerto Rican men in Milwaukee, in an iron foundry, and that those thirty-six have now expanded into a community of three thousand, entirely through family intelligence. The Migrant Division further reports that one Puerto Rican in Haverstraw, New York, has multiplied himself by nine hundred. The original Puerto Rican was an army buddy of a garageman's son in Haverstraw. A few years ago the son recommended him to the father as a handy man with a jeep, and he was sent for from the island. He turned out well, and before long he sent for his brother to come and work in a neighboring garage. One thing led to another in this way, until at last report there are nine hundred Puerto Ricans in Haverstraw, West Haverstraw, Nyack and South Nyack—manning a big junkyard and a plastics factory among other things. They have all come from the same *barrio*, or locality, on the island.

Elsewhere in the United States this same phenomenon, more or less, has occurred. There is a large Puerto Rican community in Lorain, Ohio, and 75 percent of its members are said to have relatives there or in some other American city. And in Cleveland there are about four thousand Puerto Ricans, who are said to share only a handful of family names between them.

I got a glimpse of how this process looks from the other end, too, when I was in Puerto Rico. I met an old man there, on the south coast, who was a sugar-worker and who had employment only during the harvest, or for about six months each year. Normally he would have been a poor man, with little hope of anything else for himself or his descendants. But in fact he had eleven children, and five of them—sons—were in the States with good jobs, and each with a wife and children of his own. Later it was expected that others of the children would go too, and that the older brothers would place them well and show them the ropes.

Air transport gives the Puerto Rican migration a tentative quality that the old European waves of immigrants to this country never had. The Irish, Germans, Italians, and Jews came in ships and came to stay. But most Puerto Ricans, one usually hears, come with the intent of leaving again soon—

perhaps of taking enough money back to buy a *finca*, or little farm, on the island and settle down. Often they get stuck here, of course. They earn more money in New York, but they find more ways of spending it too. They get entangled in modern appliances, bought on the installment plan, and never save the capital to go back in the style they would like. In recent months I have met two or three Puerto Rican taxi drivers who have told me they have been in New York for several years, and have complained that they can't possibly afford to go home now, though they had once hoped to. Other Puerto Ricans *do* go home, but go more empty-handed than they had planned.

Just how many Puerto Ricans—and of what age and sex —come and go is not exactly known. The standard way of checking on the migration is to watch the volume of "thrift"-class plane passages between San Juan and Idlewild. Thrift class in the air corresponds to steerage on the sea. It costs $52.50 one way and is the lowest of three classes available on the San Juan run—the others being "first" and "tourist." It is assumed that ordinary Puerto Rican migrants use this class and that few other people do. So by subtracting the southbound thrift traffic from the northbound, statisticians feel they can estimate the "net" migration.

In 1956, by this reckoning, five out of every six Puerto Ricans who came up went back, and only one stayed. Actually the movement wasn't as simple as that, but had its peculiarities. For one thing there seem to have been a great many children among those who went back—being sent down to spend the summer vacation, or a longer period, with relatives, much as Negro children are often sent from New York to the South. Shuttling grandmothers form another category that figures in both the northward and southward streams; one often hears about them; they fly back and forth between their descendants at home and in New York, moved by considerations of where the freshest welcome is at the moment, say, or who needs help with a new baby.

Then there are workers who have a yearly cycle of migration. The Puerto Rican sugar harvest lasts from winter into late spring. It is possible to work through it and then to come up and work through the farm, fruit, and garden harvests of the Northeast United States, and many Puerto Ricans do that. Others work part of the year in sugar, and the rest in some New York City job—washing dishes, or making costume jewelry.

Still others just plain go home for Christmas, a time of festivity on the island and of bitter cold in New York—in the late fall weeks the net migration is nearly always minus or southward, according to the experts. It takes less than a week's good pay to fly back to Puerto Rico, and some migrants do it on slight provocation—perhaps because their health is bad, or because they have been laid off the payroll for a while.

Aside from travelers like this, who can almost be described as commuters, there are many Puerto Ricans who come up for only a year or two and then go back, perhaps to return here again, perhaps not. "Tackling New York," one man told me in San Juan, "has come to be a sort of initiation, or adventure, that many people here think they should go through. They get prestige from it. It gives them something to talk about when they come home, and usually a man can earn better pay here, too, if he has a little mainland experience. In a way it is like going to college."

My informant paused and thought for a moment. "The migration has changed a lot, you know, in the past ten years," he went on. "In '46 a Puerto Rican went to New

York as an unknown place, but in '57 he goes to it as a place where he has relatives living, and about which he has learned a lot from hearing stories in his village." He paused again. "Of course there is one thing," he said, "that Puerto Ricans cannot learn about unless they experience it, and that is the cold. Time and again I have tried to explain the cold to would-be migrants, and warn them about it. But they can't get my meaning if they have never been off this island."

New York is the capital of the world in the migrants' eyes. It is the only spot that many of them think of coming to. A few years ago a research team made a poll of New York Puerto Ricans, and a vast majority said they would rather have stayed home than migrate to any other place. The Puerto Rican government urges its people to try other parts of America, but has not had spectacular success. New York is the true metropolis, or mother city, where they are concerned.

There seem to be various reasons for this. New York is traditionally the port of entry for Puerto Rico. The ships always came to it from the island, and they went from it too, bearing exports—all good things began in New York harbor, so to speak. Now, of course, the planes come in to Idlewild, and the location of that field affects the passengers' destination.

Then New York has the bright lights. It is the scene of many wonders that Puerto Ricans see on the screen or hear about on the radio. It draws them as it has drawn the farm boys of the forty-eight states. Even the sad encounters with reality that Puerto Ricans often have in New York don't seem to hurt the city's reputation too much at home. The migrants forget about such things when they go back there, and tell instead of their adventures in Times Square.

In a way New York is the metropolis of the whole Atlantic and Caribbean, and it might draw people from all the islands if national boundaries didn't prevent. In the 'twenties and 'thirties, natives of the Western Hemisphere were not excluded by our immigration laws, and a great many British West Indian Negroes came to New York then. A number of them settled in Harlem and became landlords there, being rather unpopular with the domestic Negroes for this reason and because they were thought high hat— they were Episcopalians and relatively well-educated. Many Cubans came in those years too, along with other Spanish-speaking Caribbeans and not a few Haitians—I met one of these Haitians in New York a while ago, when visiting a factory that employed several Puerto Ricans; he said he lived among Puerto Ricans himself in East Harlem, and had learned to speak Spanish (not to mention English) besides his native creole patois.

Nowadays, though, with the McCarran-Walter Act, few outsiders can enter our country, and the British West Indians have been going to London, Birmingham, and other English industrial centers, where they are creating a stir rather like that caused by the Puerto Ricans here—though their migration is in much smaller volume, because of the longer distance, and is confined much more to single adult males. The influx to New York has pretty well thinned down to Puerto Ricans, who are American citizens with full rights, even though they are not in the continental United States and don't belong to a state.

Their anomalous position has, incidentally, led to some fine points of semantics. They are tempted to refer to the mainland and mainlanders as America and Americans, because it is so easy, and they sometimes do this, though on principle they prefer not to, for they are Americans themselves—real United States ones—and proud of it for the most part. To get round this mistake, therefore, they are apt to say "the States" when speaking of the mainland, and to use "continental" as an adjective for mainland persons, customs, and so forth. "Mainland" itself they use too, but principally when some idea of physical location is involved —they will speak, for instance, of the mainland plant or office of some firm, as opposed to the island one. Themselves they call simply Puerto Ricans or Puertoriqueños, except in flowery or sentimental contexts, when they often say Borinqueños for themselves and Borinquen or Boricua for their island—these words, which come from the name of their Indian predecessors, are common on Puerto Rican shop-signs in New York.

One other term used for Puerto Rico, especially in politics, is "The Commonwealth." This comes from "Associated Commonwealth of Puerto Rico," the island's rather cumbrous official name. After we took Puerto Rico in 1898, there were two main lines on which politicians there could agitate—they could demand either freedom or statehood. A goodly number did each, and two political parties started up accordingly, but neither won out and both are far behind in the race now. They have been distanced by still a third party, that of Governor Luis Muñoz Marín, which appeals less than the first two to the island's pride, perhaps, but more to its economic needs.

Muñoz argues that freedom would be impossible for Puerto Ricans now because they would then all be pent up on their overcrowded island with no migration, and no outside investments, to ease their plight. Statehood would be equally bad, he points out, because then Puerto Rico would have to pay federal taxes, like its forty-eight sisters, and it could not afford this. As an alternative he and his colleagues, with Washington's help, have worked out the "Associated Commonwealth" idea, which keeps the island inside United States territory—thereby securing a free flow of migrants and capital between it and the mainland—but gives it no true representation in, and conversely no taxation by, the federal government.

So far Muñoz's policy has done well, and the Puerto Ricans are sold on it. His party has an overwhelming majority, and he is virtually an all powerful ruler of the island —a modern, enlightened version of the old Spanish autocrat.

When I was in Puerto Rico I rented a car, and took out a driver's license and with it some insurance. "Will this cover me in everything?" I asked the driver who arranged it. "What will happen if I run over the governor, for instance?"

The driver looked blank a moment and then burst into smiles. "Oh, you don't have to worry about that," he said, "because you will be killed right away."

Muñoz is an arresting personality. He has a big nose, big ears, and a small moustache, and looks rather like the Mexicans one sees in cartoons. He comes from the small minority of well-educated Puerto Ricans—both his father and his mother were accomplished political leaders before him—and he is usually credited with a fine, sophisticated mind. He is a poet, among other things, and expresses himself trenchantly in English, and presumably in Spanish too —his metaphors, especially, are vivid and evocative.

His political style is new-dealish. He first won a majority in the legislature at about the time Tugwell became governor of the island in 1941, and from then on he has been the chief political force there, though he didn't become gov-

ernor himself till 1949, under a new constitution that gave
Puerto Ricans a larger degree of self-rule. During all this
period—and before it—he has been building up a brain-
trust that impresses most visitors with its high sense of
mission and with the air of going places that it imparts to
the island.

The member of this group who is best known in New
York, perhaps—aside from Muñoz himself—is Doña Felisa
Rincón de Gautier, the mayoress of San Juan. Doña Felisa
is a distinguished-looking woman, with aquiline features
and blue-gray hair that she augments with a switch and
stacks in handsome coiled braids atop her head, sometimes
backing these up with a splash of white feathers. She
dresses smartly and has a twinkle in her eye.

Once I watched her at a rally, in Madison Square Garden, of District 65, a New York union local of workers in
department stores and related enterprises, which has many
Puerto Rican members. She sat on the platform with a
group that included dozens of Negro, Puerto Rican, Jewish,
and other labor leaders—and eventually Governor Harriman as well. The program offered speeches and also a small
band of zany rock-and-roll musicians, who played while
standing on their heads and generally clowned around on
the stage's front edge. During these events Doña Felisa
registered surprise at times, but always poise and good
humor too. And she made a speech herself, in nearly perfect
English, in the course of which she urged her countrymen
who were present to "do everything you possible can for
the good name of Puerto Rico."

During the next few days, in New York's Spanish press,
I saw pictures of Doña Felisa visiting plants in New Jersey
and other suburbs where Puerto Ricans are employed. She
looked a good deal like Mrs. Roosevelt in this role, but with

more of a lilt to her, and she gave a fine impression of the leadership her government holds out to its migrants.

Operation Bootstrap may make or break the Muñoz regime, according to how it fares. It is a novel and inspiring enterprise. Its origins go back to the war, when the Puerto Rican government made a fat income from, among other things, rum sales to the thirsty mainland. The government decided to reinvest these profits mainly in utilities, including power, and in heavy industries, including cement plants. This was the new economic policy's first phase, and it ended when Puerto Rico's planners decided that too much government in industry was bad—the government by itself couldn't command nearly all the capital needed by Puerto Rico, they figured, and besides, by running so many plants, it found itself opposed to labor in an embarrassing way.

The next phase, in which Operation Bootstrap really developed, leaned heavily on the island's immunity from federal taxes—it sought to lure all kinds of light industries there with this inducement, besides those of cheap labor and cheap factory sites. It did nicely in several fields, the most noteworthy being some of the smaller clothing trades —I was told in Puerto Rico, for instance, that 86 percent of America's brassières are now made there.

But even this was not enough for the planners, who felt that the new influx was miscellaneous and might prove impermanent, and who therefore launched the third phase, which aims at "industrial integration." Under this phase a big new oil refinery (mainland owned) is being put up on the island's south coast, and near it a still more costly "petrochemical" plant is contemplated—one that will make industrial chemicals from the refinery's output. Plastics and synthetics factories will all follow, according to the planners, who are optimistic about the new trend—one of them, a mainlander, even predicted when I was in Puerto Rico that the island might have full employment by 1965.

He felt that conditions down there were very favorable. The new industries were integrated with the mainland, for one thing—this meant that Puerto Rico belonged to a big economic unit, which he said was almost a necessity for high development these days. For another thing, he said the prestige of economic planning was especially high in Puerto Rico, partly because Muñoz had such firm political control, and partly because the island's Spanish traditions gave much less power to private enterprise than the latter enjoyed on the mainland. For this reason Puerto Rican officials threw themselves into planning with a will, he said, and he felt they were more sophisticated about economics than similar officials on the mainland would be.

These dreams of a bright future postulate at least two things—continued prosperity on the mainland, and continued good will here toward Puerto Rico. The prosperity is in the lap of the gods, but the good will could be upset by various tangible, foreseeable events, such as further attempts by Puerto Rican extremists to shoot the President or the Congress, further charges that Red propaganda is being disseminated here from Puerto Rico, or further scandals about the migrants in New York and other cities.

To head the last of these off—and to save the island's good name generally—the Puerto Rican Labor Department takes great pains over the migration both here and at home. It directly runs the movement of about fifteen thousand contract workers to the mainland and back each year— they come chiefly for harvest jobs—and it seeks to influence the other migrants too. It goes about this by assuming that everyone of the island is a potential migrant, or *migrante*, and by trying to indoctrinate the whole populace. It aims at keeping people up to date on the employment situation here—if the garment industry is laying off workers, for instance, it gets on the radio and says so. It also advises Puerto Ricans about things like garbage disposal in New York, and about how to hang their laundry on lines instead of just draping it out their windows.

The Puerto Rican government claims to have a laissez-faire policy toward migrants, and to let them go wherever they wish; but its officials do admit to steering them away from the South, for instance, by telling them about segregation there, and to getting as many of them as possible to leap over New York, instead of settling there and further crowding the Puerto Rican ghettos.

Up here on the mainland, the Labor Department's migrant office continues to serve the *migrantes*, helping them to get jobs, helping them to know their rights under the housing laws, and so forth. The principal migrant office is in New York City, and there are branches throughout the Northeast and as far west as Chicago.

Our exchange of influence with Puerto Rico is a two-way thing. Besides the factories that have gone down there, the island has a big tourist business now, with huge hotels that act as beachheads of mainland culture, or at least of its more lurid side. There has also been a southward migration of New Yorkers. When I was in San Juan a party was held at my hotel by the local Jewish Community Center. Hundreds of members turned out, and on enquiring I was told that they had all, or nearly all, moved to the island recently, along with the garment trade. If such things keep up, New York and Puerto Rico may be almost the same in a few decades, except for climate. But meanwhile they are different—very different—and the migration continues.

III *Among the Cold People*

Flight 298—thrift class—of Pan American Airways leaves San Juan at 3 p.m. on weekdays, jam-packed with Puerto Ricans. Each plane on the run can carry 106 passengers, and extra planes, or "sections," are added as need be. They climb into the blue tropical heaven and set their noses for New York, 1,600 miles away. They drone on, and the blue becomes the black Atlantic night; then about 8 p.m. they make the lights of Idlewild and come down. At the airport a sea of other Puerto Ricans is waiting, and they sweep the newcomers off to crannies in the city.

I flew up from San Juan on flight 298, after my visit there, and my Puerto Rican fellow-passengers were able-bodied men for the most part. (Two weeks earlier I had flown south, by thrift class too, and then the passengers had been mainly women and children; there had been some twenty babes in arms aboard, and the plane had sounded like a maternity-ward nursery.) Most of the men on this plane coming up looked like outdoorsmen, with weather-beaten faces and wrinkled necks, and when we were under way they began talking loudly with each other, and with some of the women and children aboard. Usually passengers on planes are subdued and silent, in my experience, but not so these Puerto Ricans. They expressed themselves freely and made the most of the adventure, and by three hours out there was a real hubbub.

At about that time, too, the passengers began putting on warm clothes and getting ready for the new environment. I remember a woman putting woolen trousers, with suspenders, on a little girl. She somehow got them on under the girl's flounced petticoat and flaring red skirt, but in general the passengers put their warm things *over* what they had started with. This had a snuffing-out effect. The light, bright clothes of the tropics were obscured by the drab ones of the north, and the crowd getting off the plane looked different from the one that had got on it.

The Puerto Ricans meeting us were dressed in the northern way, of course, and to judge by their clothes they belonged to several different levels of prosperity. There were scores or hundreds of them there—lots of children, lots of women with scarves on their heads—and they embraced the newcomers and stood round chatting. Then we went our ways—I to a warm hearth in my native city, they to their strange, forbidding slums.

"They go to a certain part of the city because they have friends or relatives there," a Puerto Rican—long accustomed to New York—told me later. "The friends meet them at Idlewild and take them in to live with them. The next thing is to find a job, and a friend can help there too. He will take the new man to the factory or wherever else he's working. That's the first approach, and if it doesn't succeed he'll try something else. In general he will know which factories are taking on help. For instance, in parts of the summer, the garment industry is busy on fall and winter wear. Then in the fall the toy factories are going great guns, and the makers of jewelry and novelties. There are lots of others too, and with any luck he should get a job soon.

"Next, he should find a place to live. He really should leave his friend after a reasonable time, and he may want to bring his family up as well. Finding a place isn't easy, and in the end he will probably have to settle for a dump and pay good money for it. That will be just part of his troubles, though. He will have to get used to the rush-rush-rush here—to getting places on time. He will have to learn how to take criticism from his boss without feeling insulted. He will have to get used to the cold, and the city life, and all kinds of other things. It is a very big change."

In the past few months I have talked with many Puerto Ricans, and New Yorkers who deal with Puerto Ricans, and have usually heard the migrants' difficulties here explained on two grounds—the cultural change they go through, and the hardships of slum life itself, which are rated bad enough to affect any group subjected to them.

Experts disagree as to whether more of New York's Puerto Ricans come from the city or the country districts of their island—indeed there seems to be no sure way of settling this point, as country Puerto Ricans tend to claim city origin if asked, in the hope of seeming less like bumpkins. If a migrant has lived a long time in a big, modernized place like Ponce, Mayagüez, or the suburbs of San Juan, he will be that much more sure of himself in New York, and that much more ready to use the social services here—and to co-operate in filling out the forms that modern life demands in return. If he comes from the country, or from a brief stay in some urban shantytown, he may be almost raw material. He may not even be used to window-glass, as he has never really needed it to protect himself from nature. He may be in the habit of throwing his garbage out the door, though his government will have tried to indoctrinate him against this. He may not be used to punctuality as we understand it, or to keeping his voice down while others are trying to concentrate.

"Our Puerto Rican boys have no consciousness of time," an athletic director in a New York settlement house told me last winter. "A boy may show up half an hour late if you're taking them on an excursion, and he can't understand why the bus has left. 'Didn't I tell you I was coming?' he will say later. Or he may be ahead of time. Puerto Ricans often don't realize how much earlier the sun rises here in the summer—the day is always about the same length down there, you know—and a boy may ring your bell at six o'clock when an outing is scheduled. You ask him what he's doing, and he'll tell you it is daytime already and he thought you would be starting."

As for the failure to keep voices down—or the tendency to make noise generally—it is one of the main things that New Yorkers who live close to Puerto Ricans complain about. Signs requesting quiet are frequent in offices where Puerto Ricans congregate. One of these that I have seen— addressed to mothers visiting a baby clinic in East Harlem —shows a tact that might be used more often in such cases. "Please talk low," it says, "so the doctor can hear the babies' heart-beats." If not restrained in such ways, Puerto Ricans tend to create a babble that may be all right in their native villages, but that conflicts with many things in city life.

New Yorkers who know the Puerto Ricans well—social workers, priests, teachers, and the like—usually credit them with great warmth and generosity. "If a Puerto Rican kid has twenty cents he will usually give a dime of it to a friend," a playground director told me last fall. Puerto Rican children are also said to be very creative in music and painting. Puerto Ricans of all ages are said to be loyal if treated right—"If they like you they'll never let anything be said against you," in the words of a union organizer here who has spent much time with them on picket lines. They are said to be individualistic—"every one of them is a Don Quixote"—and almost over-sensitive to criticism.

"They care a lot about their dignity, or *dignidad*," one man who knows Puerto Ricans and other Latin Americans well has told me. "I remember once long ago, in a San Juan hotel, finding a notice in Spanish that said 'Please tell your maid not to throw her lighted cigarettes out the window; they may burn the awning below.' I couldn't understand it at first. I had no maid, nor could I imagine anyone else who would take that room having one, for it was very small. Then I figured out that the sign was really addressed to me, but in a way that wouldn't hurt my dignity."

This delicacy accounts for a habit Puerto Ricans have of saying yes to questions, whether or not they mean it, so as not to hurt the questioner's feelings. Public-health nurses in New York sometimes complain about this, saying that Puerto Ricans will listen to their instructions; will smile repeatedly and say yes, yes, they understand; and then will depart in ignorance, having taken almost nothing in.

Perhaps, according to some experts, the Puerto Ricans trust to God more than to such instructions, anyway. "Our people have faith and hope and believe that God will provide," a Puerto Rican woman has told me. "We say 'Go with God,' and 'If God wills it,' and so forth, in speaking of our everyday actions, and so perhaps we don't put much faith in man-made rules." This belief that God will provide seems to characterize many peoples who live close to nature rather than to the clock.

Puerto Ricans' ideas on sports are also different from our mainland ones, according to a Puerto Rican who works with youth movements here. "Being a good loser is a new idea to our people," this man has said. "A Puerto Rican is very proud, you know, and it is a tragedy if he loses. He'll get over it, but meanwhile he'll suffer a great deal. Abiding by the decision of a judge or referee is a new idea too, and we Latins don't accept it easily." Yet these attitudes are said to be changing because baseball is so popular in Puerto Rico, and is played so much there. Basketball is getting popular there too (and is very prevalent among New York Puerto Ricans because it takes so little space). Boxing is popular on the island, but football is not, because of the heat. Horse-racing is popular, and so is cock-fighting—often when driving through the Puerto Rican countryside on Sunday afternoons you will find legal cockpits in operation, with rather beery men sitting round them in steep tiers in the heat. Puerto Ricans have sought to bring the sport up here with them too, and occasionally a fight gets raided in some Puerto Rican suburb like Brentwood, Long Island. (It is one of the few types of lawbreaking that they import, incidentally, rather than adopting from mainland precedents.)

The language barrier is often blamed for keeping Puerto Ricans, especially adult ones, from adjusting to New York. Some adults come up here without knowing English, and don't see the need for learning it—often they don't even see the possibility of learning it, for they are not experienced in the way education can dispel ignorance, stage by stage, if one sticks to it. They are also too proud to use bad broken English. So they get a job in some shop with a Spanish-speaking straw-boss, and in their spare time they consort with other Puerto Ricans and watch the Spanish movies or Spanish TV programs. They stay in their ghettos and think about going back to their island some day.

"They get a ghetto mentality and never learn what New York has to offer," a social worker on the Lower East Side has told me. "I take some of them to Rockefeller Center, and I find that after a year here they haven't even heard of the place. Or I mention a new picture that's playing, but unless it's playing down here at the New Delancey it isn't really a picture to them."

Such complaints are against the Puerto Ricans' failure to move horizontally, so to speak, from their ghettos. Others are heard against their failure to move vertically from them—specifically, to raise themselves up by learning in the manner of earlier immigrants, most notably the Jews.

"The Jewish immigrants felt that success would come through education," a settlement house psychologist has told me, "and the Italians were somewhat the same. In the garment trade twenty years ago a high percentage of the workers had kids going through college, but this is no longer the case. A general de-emphasis on education is taking place in our society now. You don't have a ferment these days to get out of the slums by educational achievement, but by financial achievement, and the Puerto Ricans reflect this. The Puerto Rican kids here dream of quick money, not of intellectual attainments."

Much the same thing has been told by other observers. In general they have said that the Puerto Ricans here lack the high cultural concepts of the older European immigrants, especially the Jews, and that they therefore cannot see what is to be gained by striving toward such things. No doubt too much generalizing on this point is dangerous, but I do remember talking—in fluent English—with an intelligent young Puerto Rican in a garment factory last spring, and he surprised me by showing almost no ambition at all; I asked him if he was working toward some other employment, and he said no, he was happy where he was, making good pay, and not inclined to risk a change. It also must be remembered that the old Puerto Rican society is more stratified than that of the mercantile European cities from which the Jews came, and that New York's Puerto Ricans have been drawn from the lower layers of that stratification. That this makes for inhibitions goes without saying.

Anyhow, to the extent that all these bars to mobility exist, they tend to shield Puerto Ricans here from the rather formidable Americanization process that has grown up over the decades.

The mere physical adjustment of Puerto Ricans to New York makes for some problems, even if the obvious one of cold weather is overlooked.

On the average, Puerto Ricans are smaller than mainlanders, for one thing, and this works against them in certain lines of employment—stevedoring, for instance. An athletic coach in the slums once told me that Puerto Rican boys there seem to lack stamina. "They are good baseball players," he said, "and they are very interested. They are getting interested in basketball too, though one trouble there is that they're so small. They are quick at sports, but they don't seem to last long. My own idea is that it must be their diet. In baseball they are through after an hour and a half. And on swimming trips they will often beg you on the way out—in the bus—to let them stay in for three hours, but in the end they will invariably get their fill of that, too, after an hour and a half."

By and large the blame for the Puerto Ricans' small size and low stamina, to the extent that they really suffer from these things, does seem to rest on diet, or environment in general. There is some belief that heredity gets into it as well, but not much proof of this. The Puerto Ricans are descended from three main stocks, and two of these—the

Spanish and the Negro—are plainly up to normal standards in size. I have not learned whether the Borinqueños, the Indians who furnished the third principal strain, were deemed small or large when discovered by Columbus, but if they were small this too could be blamed on the Puerto Rican environment. Many cases are known, again, of a small people growing larger in one generation through dietary change. Chinese families moving to the treaty ports in their country—and thereby to a Western diet, including things like milk—have sometimes done this. So have Chinese families in America, when a given generation has been brought up on a notably more American diet than the one before it. And for that matter purely "American" families seem to be growing taller nowadays, generation by generation, as the science of diet unfolds. There seems little reason to doubt that Puerto Rican families will do the same if they stay in New York and learn to eat like New Yorkers.

The migrants' diet is often criticized for its reliance on rice and beans, but one dietician I talked with last winter defended it.

"There is nothing wrong with a good Puerto Rican diet down on the island," she said, "though a poor one may lack protein—certainly it will lack animal protein. The trouble is that Puerto Ricans stop eating some of their traditional foods when they come up here, and they don't know just what they are missing by this. They give up some of their native fruits and vegetables, for instance. It is true that they substitute other fruits and vegetables, but these aren't quite the same. Puerto Ricans here love things like canned apricot and pear juice, and canned fruit salad, but these have been subjected to heat and processing, and they have less virtue left in them than the native fruits back home. Some of those fruits are wonderful. For instance, there is the acerola, a dark-red West Indian cherry, which is the best source of Vitamin C we know of. Puerto Ricans eat it often down there, and seldom up here. They can't tell that this makes much difference, but it does."

The dietician was concerned about the Puerto Ricans' vitamin intake because, she said, they ate so many "empty calories" in the form of sweets, fats, and polished rice. I was interested in the question of polished rice especially, because I had encountered it before when living in China— by and large the Chinese whom I knew would insist on eating white, polished rice no matter how much they were lectured on the nutritional benefits of the unpolished kind— and I asked the dietician about the Puerto Ricans' reasons for such a preference. She thought it was because white rice, which is more expensive, gave "status" to the poorer people who ate it, and I dare say she was right, though I have also heard that white is associated with purity in this connection, and I know from experience that unpolished rice goes down the throat less easily than polished. Anyway, the dietician said that she did find it hard to put unpolished rice over with Puerto Ricans, and that she had better luck with "enriched" rice, though this was more expensive.

As for the beans in the Puerto Rican diet, she felt that they were a pretty good source of protein, but not a perfect one, and she explained that proteins have an "order of value," depending on their richness in essential amino acids, in which animal proteins—those from meat, eggs, milk, and fish—rate first; proteins from nuts rate second; those from peas and beans rate third; and those from cereals rate fourth. She felt that many Puerto Ricans here eat less meat than they should, from a dietary viewpoint, but that little can be done about this now, as the problem is basically economic.

So far as I have learned, incidentally, the Puerto Ricans do eat a good deal of meat, both in New York and on their island, when they can afford it. Their meat preferences differ somewhat from ours, though—they lean more toward household animals, like pigs and poultry, and less toward range animals, like beef, because their island is so crowded.

The relationship between Puerto Ricans and milk has also been studied by this dietician, and by other health authorities I have talked with. The dairy cow is a sort of queen in our culture, but traditionally she has had much less prestige in Puerto Rico, a tropical island where milk goes sour fast and where nature gives a fairly adequate living, anyway, without much prodding by man. The Puerto Ricans might have almost no dairy tradition, one gathers, except that they are given to drinking *café con leche*, or coffee with milk. Thanks to this habit, the milk consumption of Puerto Rican adults in New York—according to Health Department surveys—averages slightly more than that of the city's adults as a whole.

But the consumption by Puerto Rican children and babies here is still thought much too low, and the authorities are trying to increase it; they are trying, among other things, to persuade Puerto Rican mothers to use evaporated milk, which they believe is cheaper and more convenient. But here they are up against an ingrained prejudice that such milk is too *caliente* (literally, "hot"), an old-wives' concept that is hard for an outsider to grasp exactly, but that seems to give this milk the properties of inducing fevers and gas on the stomach, and making the skin break out. Often the nurses in the city's baby clinics advise Puerto Rican mothers to use evaporated milk, but assume that when the latter go home they will use cow's milk anyway. In general, the New York health authorities assume that many of their instructions to Puerto Rican women will be vetoed back in the latter's slum dwellings by family councils that cling to old Latin beliefs—the belief in the virtue of obesity, for instance.

One other Latin habit that works badly in New York, I have heard, is that of the large lunch. In tropical Puerto Rico the siesta has been customary—in the past, at least—and life has tended to stand still in the early afternoons. So a heavy lunch has been in order if one could afford it. But Puerto Ricans working in New York must often adopt the local habit—however barbarous—of bolting down a sandwich and rushing on again. This is all right in itself, perhaps, but it implies a larger breakfast than the traditional one of *café con leche* with a bite of bread, and so adjustments have to be made all around.

Concerning the Puerto Ricans' general health I have talked with several experts here, including Dr. Leona Baumgartner, the city's health commissioner. By and large these experts have denied that the migrants bring fell diseases to New York, as is sometimes charged. It is true, apparently, that many Puerto Ricans who come here have tuberculosis, and that traces of cancer are found in them at relatively early ages—the latter may be related to the shortness of their life span. Aside from these facts, reports of Puerto Rican ill health seem mainly to be rumors—symptomatic of misunderstanding by the rest of the community. (It should be said that such misunderstanding, and its symptoms, can work both ways. When the Salk vaccine was first introduced in New York on a large scale, word went round among the Puerto Ricans that it was a secret device for poisoning them.)

The city's hospitals see much of the Puerto Ricans; the latter flood the clinics at places like Bellevue. Not only do they suffer from tuberculosis; they also make great use, as their birth rate is so high, of the maternity and pediatrics facilities. The more rustic of them, understandably, are not much used to modern health services, and there is some trouble meshing them in with these.

One doctor I talked with a few months ago, at a privately supported hospital—not a city-owned one, that is—expressed himself tartly to me on Puerto Rican patients, and his comments may be of interest, though he admitted to being sourer than average on the subject. "The Puerto Ricans who come here don't stand pain well," he told me. "They seldom speak good English, so they can't describe their symptoms clearly, and we cannot be sure they'll take the medicine prescribed. Often they expect a good deal from us, though they have no money to pay. In pediatrics it is hard to discipline the adults who come to visit the children—lots of these come in winter, especially, because the hospital is warmer than their homes then. They bring in food despite orders not to, and sometimes they give it to children right before surgery—which is very bad, of course—and they disturb our routine in other ways too. I think our hospital should do more toward educating these adults when they come in here, as a way of teaching all the Puerto Ricans in the neighborhood about health—I believe it will take a generation or two to educate them in this regard."

The doctor told me that the Puerto Ricans, in his observation, came to New York with various ailments of poverty—malnutrition and iron deficiency, for instance—but not often with rickets or scurvy. They were apt to have intestinal worms when they arrived, but could not infect others here with them because of the urban sanitary system, which is so different from the latrineless outdoors of their homeland. The doctor remarked on their high incidence of tuberculosis, and said a suggestion had often been made that they be required to pass a chest x-ray in San Juan before flying up here. Aside from these particular diseases, he said, the Puerto Ricans seemed to have only the usual ones, and in the usual degree.

He freely admitted, incidentally, that Puerto Rican labor was needed by his hospital, though he wasn't too complimentary about it. "We always get the dregs of the labor market," he said. "In 1944, when I first came here, we had the least employable of the Irishmen in New York. Now we have the Puerto Ricans. I don't think that they are very competent, but I also don't think we could get along without them."

This doctor said frankly that he had little rapport with the Puerto Ricans, and that his views on them were probably biased. He was, so to speak, objective about his non-objectivity, and I welcomed his words as a counter to what I had been hearing from city officials, who I feared might be biased on the other side. (The conditions the doctor referred to, of course, are also found—to the extent that he described them accurately—in Bellevue and other city hospitals.)

Last winter, too, I visited a few "well-baby" clinics, run by the city's Department of Health, in the Puerto Rican districts. The function of these clinics is to check on the neighborhood babies' health periodically—to weigh them and so forth—and to coach the mothers in their feeding and care. It was bitter cold weather when I made these visits, and the Puerto Rican mothers would come in all bundled up, with scarves on their heads. The babies would be bundled up too, in cocoons of blankets—occasionally they would look like bundles, pure and simple, without any hint of the babies inside them. The mothers would sit and hold them, in rows on benches, awaiting their turn, and the room would be full of babies' cries, echoing back and forth on the bare walls. The nurses in the clinics could rarely speak Spanish, and they would instruct the mothers through pidgin English and baby talk, repeatedly using gestures too—"I often say that if I broke both my arms I'd be useless here," one of them told me one day.

The nurses would question the mothers about their use of orange-juice, milk, vitamins and cereal. They would give bits of advice, not sure if these would be heeded or even understood. "If you have cold, and you kiss, then you give cold to the little baby," a nurse would say. The mother would smile and smile and nod her head. Then she would pick her bundle up and go outside, perhaps kissing it forthwith and covering it with germs—but perhaps also remembering something about the vitamins.

The family set-up of the migrants differs from the New York standard, and this calls for adjustments, too. Demographers, or students of population, say that the natural-increase rate of New York's Puerto Ricans is more than twice that of New York's native whites (with that of New York's Negroes falling in between). This startling figure comes in part from the fact that most Puerto Ricans in the city are in the prime of life, having come here to work. But even so, the overall increase rate of the Puerto Ricans—and their birth rate—is high.

Time and again I have heard elaborations on this theme by experts, Puerto Rican, and otherwise. They have told me, for instance, that young Puerto Ricans get interested in romance a couple of years earlier than young mainlanders; that Puerto Rican girls not uncommonly have a child or two by the time they are seventeen; and that Puerto Rican families here average at least five members—with sets of six, seven, or eight children being frequent.

Some experts believe that the Puerto Ricans' early maturity is related to the shortness of their life span—a possibility we have touched on above in connection with cancer. But their high rate of increase—a different though related matter —is usually credited to the particular stage of their culture: to the fact that they are shifting from an "underdeveloped," agrarian economy to a technologically advanced one. This shift is occuring in many parts of the world now—such as Ceylon and Formosa, to name two other islands—and a big jump in population usually goes with it. The agrarian families have customarily produced many children in the past, according to the usual explanation, but these have been thinned out drastically by infant diseases; now, however, the diseases are being stopped by modern science, and the families are expanding unchecked. This theory, which certainly seems to fit the facts, has also a corollary: that large broods of children are welcome in the old agrarian life— where they are easy to raise and will support the parents in old age—but are an embarrassment after modernization, as the rearing of each child then requires a cash outlay, and the child leaves home when grown. Modernized parents soon catch on to this difference (one usually hears), after which they often try to limit their child-bearing by late marriage, birth control and other means. It is often argued that lower-class Puerto Ricans, and especially the New York ones, are in one of the more painful phases of this process now: they are still producing in the old agrarian way, that is, but are raising their children in the expensive city—they haven't learned as yet to cope with their new situation.

Birth control is being preached in Puerto Rico, and birth-control advice is being made available there by the government of Luis Muñoz Marín. But the program faces various obstacles, the chief of them being the Catholic Church, which has a rather loose hold on its flock in Puerto Rico, by normal standards, but is nevertheless influential there. A faster spread of the birth-control idea seems likely among Puerto Ricans in New York, where striking results have already been achieved by one campaigner, an educated Puerto Rican woman who is connected with the Planned Parenthood Federation and who works through two Manhattan settlement houses, one in East Harlem and one on the Lower East Side. She calls herself a Catholic, which is a measure of the light discipline the Church exerts on some Puerto Ricans—she says she knows she is going against the Church's teaching, but has decided to do so for the good of her people as she sees it. She broadcasts weekly on Spanish radio and TV programs, and reports a keen response. When I talked with her, some time ago, she had been on TV the preceding Sunday, and she told me of two mothers who had phoned in promptly on Monday morning for appointments —one was thirty-one years old and had nine children; the other was twenty-three and had seven. She said that innumerable cases on that order had come to her—women who had been having babies year after year since their teens, with the monotonous process broken only by miscarriages. Usually they were delighted by her message, which came as a sort of revelation to them, surrounded as they were by knee-high children inadequately clothed. Several thousand migrant women had already been equipped for birth control, she told me.

She felt too that Puerto Rican women in New York were more ready for birth control than those at home because so many of them had outside jobs—in the garment trade, for instance—and found it hard to get baby-sitters in the impersonal city surroundings, which were so different from the familial ones on the island. Also, she added, the women in New York were more open to scientific arguments, and less bound by their old customs.

Many Puerto Rican matches have never been solemnized by a church or civil ceremony; one sometimes hears that a fourth to a third of all couples on the island are thus informally joined. Such unions are often called "consensual" in discussions of Puerto Rico, and the New York officialdom refers to them as "out of wedlock," or "O.W.," when recording data on children. One gathers that they are stable enough in the old Puerto Rican lower-class society, where personal relations are not sharply defined—where there is much casual adoption of poor children by relatives, for instance, and where godfathers, or *compadres,* take on almost the role of foster-parents. One gathers that there is a warm, vague communal life in that society, and that everyone gets fed somehow without stressing exact rights and obligations.

In New York, though, consensual marriages do not fit the picture so well. They clash with our bureaucratic paperwork procedures—which like all relationships to be legal, and neatly spelled out in black and white—and they sometimes, for instance, make it hard for Puerto Rican families to get into housing projects. They also prove less binding when the union is put under strain, as often happens in the transition to our society. Therefore priests and others who work with the migrants take pains to get consensual marriages solemnized if the couples are serious about them.

The chief strains on migrant unions here, it seems, come from increased cash and the raised position of women. "Puerto Ricans aren't used to handling large sums when they come up here," I have been told by a nun who works with them. "It is a big change for them to earn high wages, and it goes to their head. They get restless—very materialistic. Then if they have to live in bad surroundings—like crowded tenements—they may begin to stray, and pretty soon their homes are broken."

As for the position of women, it has been traditionally low in Puerto Rico. The wife has stayed home, the husband has been lord and master, and there has been a double standard of morality. Some Puerto Rican men can make that relationship last on the mainland, and I have heard of husbands who won't even let their wives visit the city's baby clinics without their chaperonage. But by and large, our idea of freedom for women infiltrates the Puerto Rican families—and sometimes, too, it is misinterpreted, and liberty is taken as license. The situation can be made worse if the wife earns more money in New York than the husband, as she often does. Then she has cash to spend and must plainly be away from home a lot; and no matter how great her devotion she achieves an independence that humiliates a husband used to the old ways.

A like process tends to alienate Puerto Rican children from their parents in New York, as has happened with other immigrants before. In Puerto Rico parents may be kind and indulgent, but they have much authority—especially over the daughters, perhaps in a survival of the duenna system. They can be strait-laced. Then those of them who join certain evangelical Protestant churches—as many do on reaching New York—tend to become puritanical as well, even about smoking, and to enforce this attitude on the young as much as possible. Meanwhile the latter quickly pick up our mainland beliefs in "permissiveness" toward children, and they chafe more and more under their parents' conservatism. Some parents even resist letting their children go to dances at settlement houses—which makes the latter squirm when asked "Who are you going to the party with?"

Parental authority is often challenged under such circumstances, especially if both father and mother have jobs and can't be home much. In addition, the young Puerto Ricans learn English, and New York ways, more quickly than the old. Often a little child will become the interpreter, or mediator, between his family and the city—I have visited Puerto Rican lodgings where the mother sat mutely in the background while a small daughter talked knowingly, in English, with me and the city official who was guiding me. It is natural for such children to lose respect for their parents and to stop obeying them. But they have no one else to obey, either, and they find themselves alone in the no man's land of the second-generation immigrant. All authority looks bad to them, and they start getting into mischief.

This process was explained to me rather sourly, a while ago, by a friend of European descent. "The Puerto Ricans are like my people in New York a few decades back," he said, "in that the older generation has a complete sense of authority and family. The younger ones rebel against this, inevitably. At the same time they have been subjected to the elders' views on American society, which are contemptuous to say the least. The elders have no idea of community relations as these are understood here, but only of family— outside the family it is perfectly all right to cheat anyone. The younger generation is lost amid all this. Its members don't know where they fit in, and in many cases they cannot exist—cannot have significance—unless they express themselves through crime or the appearance of crime. That gets them a little attention, at least—a little sense of identity."

A while ago, I was walking on the Lower East Side with a social worker who knows the Puerto Ricans well, especially the young ones. We met three teen-age Puerto Rican boys—healthy looking, and wearing the black leather jackets that are fashionable there. They hailed my companion warmly as we passed. "Those kids have pretty long records," he said to me a moment later. "They're going to have a tough time. There's no way to reach them, you see. I can't get them to join anything."

"They seem to like you," I said.

"Yes, they do," he answered. "They're my friends, all right. But still I can't get them into anything—they slip away."

We were walking on a slum street lined by dingy brick buildings, four or five storys high. We passed many people on the sidewalks—Puerto Ricans, Negroes, and Europeans.

We walked on some more, and my companion motioned up ahead. "There is a gang over there," he said. "There's lots of theft, and a lot of playing hookey."

We passed an intersection, and he looked down to our right. "This street is a bad one," he said. "There is a lot of dope here."

"Marijuana?" I asked.

"Yes. And gambling and prostitution too. It's a low-grade kind of prostitution, of course." The street had always been pretty bad, he told me, but it had gotten worse in the past year. "The trouble is that these kids grow up in this," he said, "and get used to it. They can't think of living any other way."

We saw a crowd farther down that street, and the social worker learned from a passerby that two gamblers had just been picked up there, and a police photo unit was on the scene. Then we started back, and after a few blocks

we saw the boys we had spoken with earlier. Now they
were crouched in a huddle on the sidewalk. They broke
this up as we drew near, and my companion said they had
been gambling, too, and didn't want to be caught at it.
"It's against the law," he said, "and of course that makes it
interesting to them."

The first signs of trouble in a boy, this social worker told
me later, are usually that he plays hookey, fights a lot, and
is disrespectful to his teachers.

"If you've got a good neighborhood center, and are in
close contact, you can spot a boy like that," he said. "Or
perhaps his parents will come themselves and tell you—if
they recognize the danger. Then you must try to meet him.
You can talk to him on the street, or you can go to his home,
or you can ask him over to play ball. Kids like a club, you
know, and you have to supply that if you are trying to help
them. Of course a club, too, can turn into a gang if it isn't
properly supervised. Even a ball-team can turn into a gang.
And once a gang is started in an area, lots of good kids have
to join it for protection. Boys get a sense of pride about
their territory, for one thing. Often they seem to think
they own the girls in it. They won't like the way someone
else will look at a girl, even. That is part of their psychology,
and the gangs fit in with it. Then of course there are evil
elements trying to form these boys into gangs. There's lots
of easy money around now, and naturally the boys want
some of it. All in all, it's an easy way of life for them to
fall into."

The main New York slums have gangs in them, by and
large, and the slums with Puerto Ricans have gangs with
Puerto Ricans. (By gangs here are meant leagues of young
people, whether warlike or peaceful, and not the adult

criminal gangs that made Chicago famous.) A gang normally has a territorial basis, and in some neighborhoods, especially where Puerto Ricans have been moving in slowly,
it may include a good number of Puerto Rican boys who
have been absorbed, peaceably, along with other nationalities. Elsewhere, though—and especially where the Puerto
Rican element is new and embattled—a gang may include
young Puerto Ricans and little else.

A good example of the latter is the Dragons, on the
Lower East Side, whose threatened war with two neighboring gangs, the Sportsmen and Enchanters, had New
York on tenterhooks for more than a week in August, 1956.
At that time, the Dragons' "turf," or territory, lay south of
Delancey Street. The Sportsmen and the Enchanters, who
were then "brother gangs," or allies, were mainly Negro,
but the Sportsmen had a large white "division," or sub-
gang. The turf of the Enchanters and Sportsmen was north
of Delancey Street, in and around the Lillian Wald housing project, and the turf of the Sportsmen's white division
was still farther north—on Tenth Street, near the Jacob
Riis housing project. The combined turfs of the three gangs
covered about a square mile, and the key point in this area
may well have been the Anglican chapel of St. Augustine,
on Henry Street, whose vicar, Father G. Kilmer Myers,
played a leading part in getting the war called off.

St. Augustine's has a difficult policy of keeping its chapel
and parish house open to members of all the gangs in the
neighborhood, and it tries to enforce a pact of no fighting
on or around its premises—that is, it tries to be a neutral
sanctuary. According to Father Myers, the pact has been
violated only twice. The first time was one evening when
a hundred and fifty young people, mainly Sportsmen and
their girls, were standing on the sidewalk in front of the

chapel after a dance in the basement, and two Puerto Rican boys appeared across the street, one of them holding a shotgun, which he proceeded to fire; he didn't hurt anyone, and he managed to get into the chapel and take refuge there. Father Myers was eventually able to cool the Sportsmen off to the point where they let him walk the boy home.

The second time was when two "junkies," or dope addicts—a Puerto Rican who was a Dragon and a Negro who was a Sportsman—began fighting in front of the chapel. In this case it was the Negro who took refuge inside. The Puerto Rican followed him in with a shotgun, but other Dragons saved the day by pulling him out before he fired it.

The trouble of August, 1956, began when two Enchanters—a Puerto Rican boy and a Jewish boy—were shot and wounded by one of the Dragons on the latter's turf. The victims were going home from a settlement-house dance, but the Dragon who shot them didn't know this and suspected that they were coming to get him; there had long been bad blood between him and the two Enchanters, and to enter a rival gang's turf is usually looked on as aggression.

Right after the shooting, Father Myers and various peacemakers, including a few other priests and some members of the city's Youth Board, went into action; they began contacting the gangs and trying to arrange talks among their leaders. Meanwhile, the Lower East Side filled up with policemen. It was feared not only that the Enchanters, the Sportsmen, and the Dragons would start rumbling, but also that their allies in the city's other slums (most gangs have such linkups) would join in or would begin attacking each other in sympathetic rumbles on their own native heaths—in Harlem, the Bronx, and Brooklyn.

In this tense atmosphere, Father Myers and his colleagues kept making the rounds of the neighborhood, working on their contacts. So did the Youth Board men, and they also arranged bus trips out of town for numerous young gang leaders, to calm them down and keep them out of trouble. As for the police, they kept the boys from assembling, or even moving around. Every day, during this period, the story was front-page news. And every day, in the August heat, life on the Lower East Side continued to be abnormal and confined.

Finally the Enchanters, Sportsmen, and Dragons got tired of having the cops on their necks and sued for peace; according to Father Myers gang boys don't like to fight much anyway. Negotiations were then begun at Trinity Church on lower Broadway, which is the parent church of St. Augustine's, and in these the various gang representatives are said to have shown great astuteness. A peace was finally arranged, and when the smoke had cleared away, the Dragons, who up to then had been a small and persecuted organization, were a feared and respected power group. The Sportsmen were also found to be strong, balancing the Dragons. The Enchanters were so chastened by their experience that they quickly stopped being a "bopping" outfit altogether and became solid citizens; they have since changed their name to the Lads' A.C. And then, early this year, the work of Father Myers and the others really paid off: the Dragons split into two clubs—the Chino Squad, for boys over sixteen, and the Sea Scouts, for younger boys—both of which have been concentrating on sports and holding peaceful meetings in St. Augustine's.

One reason for the Dragons' gain in strength—during their warlike days—was that the Puerto Rican element in that part of the Lower East Side had been growing fast. A few years earlier there had been virtually no Puerto Ricans or Negroes in that region, which was a stronghold of European immigrants, especially Jewish ones. Then the Puerto Ricans began to enter. At first the Puerto Rican youths were picked on by established gangs, but in time they met this challenge by defensive imitation—by building the Dragons up into a strong, competitive outfit.

This need for self-defense is unquestionably a main reason why Puerto Rican boys join gangs in New York. Another reason is psychological—they want a sense of solidarity.

"They can't stand by themselves," a slum priest has told me, "because individually they are so different from the in-group here. So they gang together through instability and fear, and in the gangs they are intensely loyal to each other, which gives them a feeling of security."

A third reason for Puerto Rican gangsterism, I have been told, is broken or unstable homes, which force boys to look elsewhere for "identification." Running away from home, incidentally, is said to be very common among young Puerto Ricans on the Lower East Side. No fewer than nine runaway boys came to sleep at St. Augustine's during a couple of months last fall, and nobody knows how many run away in the summer, when they can sleep out in the open.

Gangs of the New York kind do not exist in Puerto Rico, it should be said; nor is there much experience there of mugging, or gratuitous violence by young toughs. Recently, however, there has been a wave of the latter, and some Puerto Ricans blame it on migrants who have returned from our city with bad habits. In San Juan I heard an elderly writer bemoan this development. He told how he had been walking home with two friends late one evening, reciting poetry, when they had been set upon and roundly beaten by some young men. He told of an Argentine danseuse who had been slugged in the face while innocently gazing at a San Juan shop-window. And he told of passers-by in the city who had had their sleeves, and arms, slashed by a razor-blade on one of the city's street corners. He said there was no tradition for that kind of thing in Puerto Rico, and it must come from the outside. He also declared that he had had to lock his house firmly against robbers since the migrants began returning from New York, though he had never done this before.

I have asked many people in New York how much of the migrants' crime can be laid to their temperament or culture, and I have found a widespread belief, based on experience, that Puerto Ricans are excitable, and that this accounts for some of their troubles. "Here in the center one kid will push another," a settlement-house worker has told me, "and then everybody will join in at once—you'd think that Egypt had been invaded."

In investigating the Puerto Ricans one hears or reads repeatedly of crimes of passion among them—where a man may stab someone else, for instance, or even shoot up a whole family, because of a woman's inconstancy. In explanation I have heard that a *punto de honor*, or point of honor, is very important to a Puerto Rican man, and often demands action on his part. I have further heard that in the city's psychiatric wards, the Puerto Rican patients are apt to be there for doing impulsive things—for dramatic gestures, say, like the drinking of strange poisons—rather than for chronic depressions, which are more of a North European specialty. The migrants also get involved, inevitably, in the petty crimes of the slums. The young ones may become collectors for the numbers game, and the women may go into prostitution—a tendency that seems to be partly economic, partly cultural, and also partly aesthetic, as

Puerto Rican women are undoubtedly attractive to much of New York's manhood.

In a way, it is more interesting to check on the crimes that Puerto Ricans don't commit than on those they do. They don't go into commercial fraud, for one thing, or into any crime that demands complex paper work or financial juggling. Nor do they go into big systematic crime of the Al Capone or Murder Incorporated type—perhaps because they haven't been around long enough to get organized that way. They are seldom guilty of arson or extortion, or of indecent exposure or other weird sex offenses (though they do have some trouble with statutory rape, as the age of consent in New York—eighteen years—is so high for them). They are not regarded as much of a problem where intoxication is concerned, though I have heard that they often drink more in New York than on their island, perhaps because they have more cash to spend.

Many of the migrants are pretty well mired in the drug habit, though the drug traffic, like juvenile gangs, is said not to exist in the Puerto Rican island tradition. Drug addiction in the slums here follows a regular pattern. It often starts among the young people, and experts say that the latter go into it for a thrill, or to avoid seeming "chicken," rather than to relieve depression or other moodiness as an adult might do. The usual way to start is by smoking marijuana, or "pot." Next comes the sniffing of heroin, then the taking of heroin by intramuscular injections, then heroin by intravenous injections—by which time the experimenter is "hooked," or dependent on drugs, to the value of perhaps fifteen dollars a day, which often makes him a willing dope "pusher" or paid miscreant of some other kind. There is said to be much addiction of all sorts in the New York slums now—though much of it is confined to the relatively innocent marijuana—and the Puerto Ricans are in it with their neighbors.

Recently I got some idea of how the marijuana traffic works in East Harlem from an informant who has been watching it there. "You must get to know the right people," he said. "You must win their confidence little by little. The pushers—*vendedores*, they are sometimes called in Spanish—are bohemian Puerto Ricans, the kind that hang around with prostitutes instead of getting married. They have no other job; they just hang around. Pot or marijuana is called *mota* or *yerba* in Spanish, and getting it can be a time consuming job. You've got to find a pusher in some bar, give him some money, and wait 'till he comes back— if he does. One cigarette costs a dollar, or you can get three for two dollars, or twelve for five. The cigarettes are tubular, like ordinary ones, but smaller, narrower—they are called a stick or joint in English, or a *tubo* in Spanish. The butt end is roach in English, or *mejoral* in Spanish. The cigarette you get may be pure marijuana or it may be tobacco and marijuana mixed—sometimes they put pepper in to fake the hot marijuana taste. When you first start smoking you can pass right out on one, two, or three cigarettes. If you get some good marijuana and smoke it scientifically, you get a skullcap or wig sensation round the top of your head. Your memory fails, too—it is very hard to find things you were sure you had about your person. You think only of pleasures of the moment, and your sensory perceptions are sharpened, not blurred over as with liquor. You feel optimistic in general. You can expect a hangover, though— it may be partly from lack of sleep. You will feel jittery, with a tendency toward nervousness and irritability, and your eyes will be oversensitive to light."

My informant didn't think, incidentally, that marijuana

was necessarily habit forming, or that it had to lead on to heroin. He said there were many Puerto Ricans who smoked in East Harlem, but that they were a small fraction of the total Puerto Rican community there. The Puerto Ricans had learned the habit from the Negroes, he said, and it was also basic to the Mexicans in Texas—to the bohemian, anti-social element among them, that is.

All in all, one gathers from the experts that Puerto Rican misdeeds in New York are caused mainly by the slum surroundings. "Most people feel that none of these things is very racial," I have been told by a man in the district attorney's office. "If you changed the environment the rest would change too." And I have heard the same from many others. Some types of crime are endemic in the New York slums, it seems, and are practiced by whoever is living there at the moment. And then there is the anti-social state of mind. Even among our rich families there are individuals, especially young ones, who don't like society's customs and who protest by misbehaving in one way or another. It is hardly surprising that such protest should be still more common in the slums.

Finally, it is said, a special amount of protest is invoked among the Puerto Ricans by the New York police, whom the former often regard as a hostile, alien group imposing the white man's law on the dark, under-privileged outsiders. Partly for this reason, excitable crowds of Puerto Ricans often gather when the police are making an arrest in one of their ghettos. Sometimes the police invite such excitement through brutality, and sometimes they don't; yet they get it anyway, and it leads to trouble.

Puerto Ricans have certain things they say about New

York. "*Hace much frío*"—"It is very cold"—is one. "*La gente es fría*"—"The people are cold"—is another. "The people never smile" is a third. This sense of coldness—both literal and figurative—comes naturally to the migrants. They have left a balmy isle where people are warmly inclined toward each other—or sometimes hotly disinclined, for brief intervals—and in New York they find, or think they find, little but cool northern hostility.

They find it most obviously, perhaps, among the strangers in the slums that they move into—most notably among the older immigrants and Negroes. The Irish on the West Side give the Puerto Ricans a bad time—as when three Irish boys blew up a bar on Christmas Eve a few years back, to hurt some Puerto Ricans in it. The Italians in East Harlem give them a bad time too—the Italian youths in Benjamin Franklin High School, at 116th Street and the East River, are said to keep the Puerto Ricans there constantly, if mildly, terrorized.

Non-slum, non-immigrant New Yorkers are often contemptuous of Puerto Ricans too, of course, and the latter realize this—a poll of New York Puerto Ricans has shown that many of them believe they are disliked and thought inferior. This contempt is something new to them, and it confuses them. I have heard one educated Puerto Rican argue that it comes largely from the propaganda against Congressman Marcantonio—the New York press went after Marcantonio, my friend points out, because of his Communist leanings, and one of its best lines of attack was to smear the Puerto Ricans, with whom he was closely identified as a patron. This campaign does indeed seem to be one reason for the contempt, though perhaps only one in many.

Anyway, the reasons are all, or nearly all, mystifying to the Puerto Ricans themselves, who explain them on the grounds that *la gente es fría,* and who build up a strong resentment in answer. The resentment is supposed to be one reason why they wear zoot suits—as a defiant symbol of non-conformity—and one reason why they are sometimes loath to communicate. "If a kid likes you he speaks English," a psychologist working with Puerto Ricans has told me. "If not he rattles away in Spanish, especially if there is a crowd present. It's his way of showing that you're an outsider." The jive talk of Negroes fills somewhat the same role, according to this psychologist—it is the defensive code of an embattled, resentful minority.

Not long ago I talked, over coffee, with an elderly, thoughtful Puerto Rican in the New York labor movement. "The Puerto Ricans come up here," he said, "and find that the people speak a different language. The food is different. The houses are different. The atmosphere in general is different. We can't say the Puerto Ricans don't like the New York culture, but they don't understand it. Sometimes they adapt to it, but often they don't. They find some kind of coldness, and naturally through that they develop sometimes hatred, sometimes an inferiority complex. If they develop an inferiority complex you see them walking through the streets afraid of everything. If they develop hatred they go sort of crazy. . ."

The old man thought a minute. "If you could see a few scenes here you would say these people are savages," he finally observed. "But in Puerto Rico you won't find any savages."

IV *The Welfare City*

New York is a house of many mansions, with much going on in them; and the Puerto Rican guests are spread through it all unevenly. They do not often deal on the Stock Exchange or go to Broadway openings; but in great numbers they prepare the city's food, and carry its messages, and play ball games in its parks. They are also well known to the officialdom. New York may be the world's prime example of a welfare state now—at least it is the richest, in value bestowed on each recipient. One way to gauge it in this regard is to take the Manhattan phone book and read the listings under "New York–City of" (three pages, mainly of welfare, educational, and law enforcement agencies); then take the Red Book and read the listings under "Social Service Organizations" and "Social Settlements" (more than two pages between them). From this a picture emerges of a huge and complex eleemosynary set-up. It has been built in the past century and more, as the idea has grown that the "haves" in a community are obligated to the "have-nots," and can best discharge their debt through institutions. And the Puerto Ricans, though reared on a warm island close to nature, are beneficiaries of the set-up through their presence in it. They have the same rights as all New Yorkers to public schooling, housing, doctoring, and other boons of the new city world, even if it is a world they did not make and don't quite understand.

Some Puerto Rican migrants fit poorly into our system of bureaucratic paperwork. Even their names can be against it. In Spanish nomenclature the mother's maiden name plays a big part. Puerto Rico's governor, for instance, is named Luis Muñoz Marín, and in this series "Muñoz" is his father's family name, corresponding to the last name in our usage; "Marín" is his mother's name, and is attached but lightly to the rest—it isn't handed down to the next generation, and it isn't used where one name stands alone: the governor is not Señor Marín, that is, but Señor Muñoz. This custom has helped confuse the New York City records, especially in the migration's early days, when a child could well be listed under different parents' names with different agencies.

Nor is that all. The poorer and more rustic migrants are apt to change their names at will. "Often a man will sign with a nickname," I have been told by an educated Puerto Rican. "His name will be Francisco, but he will write Pancho on some form, and the clerk won't know it is the same thing. Or a boy will move to a new part of the city, and people there will start calling him something else, and he will become that. Our country people don't care too much about names, anyway. A baby's parents will give it a name, but then they may stay home on the day it is christened, and the god-parents may think up something else in church—the saint's name whose day it is, for instance. After that the child has two names, and can change back and forth between them. He doesn't care. He knows he's the same person either way." But he is not the same person either way to the punch-card machines that link our government and citizens.

One hears that many Puerto Ricans, and especially the more illiterate ones, miss the point of official paperwork; they see no significance or use in it. "And some of these forms are ridiculous in the circumstances," a Puerto Rican social worker told me last winter. "They ask a man all kinds of crazy things. To list all the assets he owns—or has ever owned. To list everything he derives income from—or has ever derived it from. Questions like that are meaningless when a man has never owned anything but a hut he built himself from old boards. He finds that if he answers the questions he gets deeper and deeper into trouble, so he learns to dummy up and not tell the whole story. Of course that's likely to hurt him, really—to ruin his chances, say, of getting into a housing project."

The common-law nature of many Puerto Ricans' marriages makes trouble with the red tape, too, and so does their informal way of adopting children. They are fond of children and are given to taking them in readily; a waif in Puerto Rico can usually count on finding a home just through kindness—"There are lots of orphans there, but practically no orphanages," as one man has expressed it to me. But New York frowns on such free and easy ways, having many legal safeguards, in its impersonal society, to protect children from adults, so that adoption can be a big operation here if done by the rules. The Puerto Ricans tend to look on the safeguards, and their enforcement, as hostile measures aimed at breaking up their happy homes, and this is one more reason for them to be secretive, and to shun paperwork.

Recently a labor organizer told me that he had offered to solve income-tax problems for Puerto Ricans in his union, and that six hundred of them had taken him up. Most of them found they had money coming back to them, he said, and he added that about half the Puerto Ricans he knew of never filed tax returns at all. The tax people, incidentally, were glad to learn of his project and sent a Spanish-speaking man around from their office to help him.

All in all, the task of mediating between Puerto Ricans

and the New York red tape is a colossal one. I have talked with scores of people in New York who deal with Puerto Ricans, and I have found that nearly all of them—priests, nurses, teachers et cetera—spend much of their time explaining government procedures to the strangers. I have also found that most city officials who work with Puerto Ricans are well disposed to them, even if rather tried by their lack of sophistication. Lower officials respond in a friendly way to the Puerto Ricans' essentially warm nature. So do higher ones, and the latter also take a statesmanlike (or politicianly) stand against the prejudice that Puerto Ricans suffer from here.

Most of the higher officials, furthermore, and some of the lower ones too, have made holiday pilgrimages to Puerto Rico and have been well received by corresponding officials down there. As a result there is almost a cult of Puerto Rican lovers in the city government—rather at variance, it is, with the general New York feeling on the subject.

One place where the city touches Puerto Ricans especially is in the matter of relief or welfare, sometimes euphemistically called "public assistance." Puerto Ricans get roughly 20 percent of New York's outlay in this. One often hears that they fly up with relief as their objective, but Henry L. McCarthy, the city's commissioner of welfare, denies this report as a "canard." He declares that they come here for jobs and rarely get on relief in their first year—also that the relief money spent on them, per capita, differs but little from that spent on the city's Negroes.

The categories of relief most usually given to Puerto Ricans are "home relief" and "aid to dependent children" (as distinct from "old-age assistance," "aid to the disabled," and so forth). This comes about through the nature of their families. Not uncommonly a Puerto Rican household here will include half a dozen little children, or more mouths than can be fed on the earnings of one breadwinner in the city's low wage brackets; the difference is then made up by supplementary grants under the title of "home relief," in line with the welfare state dictum that no one shall starve.

"Aid to dependent children" (or "A.D.C.") goes normally, on the other hand, to single parents with children at home but with no breadwinners there—it is considered a cheaper, and more human, way for the state to rear such children than putting them in orphanages. Since many unions between Puerto Ricans are both prolific and unstable, it is common to find women of their community living in this way, without men but with broods of little children, perhaps by different fathers. Such households are naturals for A.D.C.

Furthermore, there is a temptation to fake the pattern by having the man of a household leave it if he is not earning much money—in which case desertion is almost the part of chivalry—or by having him merely pretend to leave it while actually staying around but hiding out when the Welfare Department's inspector comes. The Department recognizes that much A.D.C. is drawn fraudulently this way by Puerto Ricans. It tries to check on such cases, when tipped off about them, by staging early morning visitations, at five o'clock, when the man is most likely to be home. Some New York social workers frown on this practice, saying it smacks of Gestapo tactics, but it remains Welfare Department policy anyway, and it helps to keep the rolls down.

The drawing of A.D.C. can doubtless, in many cases, be called sheer parasitism on New York City, for the children concerned might better be in their ancestral Puerto Rican homes. One reason they are not there, of course, is that the island's living standards—and hence its relief standards—are low; and some experts blame this on neglect by our federal government. They say that Washington has never done its duty by Puerto Rico—and is even now spending far less money there, than say, in Mississippi—and that New York, unluckily, must bear the burden. The point seems a fair one, though it is mitigated by the fact that Washington pays about a third of New York's relief bill—another third being paid by Albany, more or less, and the rest by the city itself.

The "home relief" drain seems less parasitic, from the city's view. It goes to real workers, by and large, and they claim it because private industry doesn't support them on the scale the welfare state deems suitable in this time and place. That scale is a high one, by any other standard. When I checked in 1956, I learned that the average grant to relief cases in New York was almost a hundred dollars a month. Many of these cases, it is true, were large households without other means of support. But many, too, were single individuals, and many were receiving only small supplementary grants.

Housing is another boon of the welfare state in New York, but one that is less fully in the Puerto Ricans' grasp. Recently the New York City Housing Authority said it had about ninety-three thousand families in its various "projects." Of these, 46 percent were white, 39 percent were Negro, and only 15 percent were Puerto Rican—"white," "Negro" (or "non-white") and "Puerto Rican" being the three main classes into which the city was dividing its people at that time.

These figures mean that the Puerto Ricans are getting only about half as much public housing, per capita, as the Negroes. One reason is that they have not been here as long—two years of residence are demanded by the rules. Another is their language problem, and their allergy to paper forms. A third is the frequent informality of their unions; stable families are preferred in the housing projects. A marriage certificate is a good way to show such stability, but often a Puerto Rican couple can't produce one; often, indeed, a couple will choose not to seem stably mated so the woman can draw A.D.C.—and which way to play this game is said to be a hard dilemma for many slum Puerto Rican households now.

Finally, a number of Puerto Rican families are kept out of projects by being too big; the Housing Authority—in order to maintain its standards—usually insists on a limit of two people per bedroom in its quarters, and, paradoxically, this will often keep a big family from leaving, say, a two-room private flat for a four-room public one; in which case the family will have to wait, in some bewilderment, till a still bigger project flat becomes available.

In truth, the migrants are badly served for housing. They are penned up in overcrowded ghettos (though less so than the Negroes are, once they have learned the ropes). They must often "pay Park Avenue rents for miserable slums," as one social worker has put it. Usually they find only run down housing available, and they run it down further by their tendency to crowd together and neglect the sanitary side. Often they have to "buy" their flats or rooms, though this is illegal: they have to make a down payment, that is—ostensibly, perhaps, for some token furniture— before they can move in and start paying the exorbitant rent.

"They might have to pay two hundred dollars for a chair like that," I was told one day in the New York State Rent Commission office—the chair, in which I was sitting, was a simple straight one. "Or they will pay a few hundred for junk that the Salvation Army wouldn't touch if you tried to give it to them. There's a law against selling a used mattress in this city, but these landlords don't hesitate to sell one—one about ready to walk out the door—to take wings."

And then the Puerto Rican tenant, having bought his wretched diggings, is liable to be forced out of them a few weeks later. This, too, is illegal, but there are tricks to the trade. I have heard, for instance, of one landlord who simply disconnected a tenant's electricity, in hopes of forcing him out. That case went to court, it happened, and the landlord was made to turn the lights back on, but many another man has gotten away with such tactics.

The business of preying on Puerto Rican tenants here—often done, regrettably, by other Puerto Ricans who have learned their way around—is said to be very profitable. This is especially true with old one-family dwellings or apartment houses—"railroad"-apartment houses, for instance—that have been cut up into single rooms, skimpily furnished. A four-story building of this sort may well bring in a thousand dollars a month, with very little outlay and very little work on the landlord's part, aside from that of bleeding the tenants regularly.

The Temporary State Housing Rent Commission is supposed to stop overcharges and other violations, but it has 1,800,000 family dwellings theoretically under rent control in the city, which means that it simply cannot seek the evils out, but must wait for complaints to come in about them. The Puerto Ricans suffer from this especially, being slow to complain because they don't know their rights and often can't speak English. Besides, they are easily intimidated by their landlords or "supers," fearing they will be evicted if they talk out of turn—I have even heard of supers who throw out mail that comes for their Puerto Rican tenants from the government housing agencies.

Because of all this a number of "rent clinics," offering free expert advice, have been started in the Puerto Rican sections of town, at settlement houses, churches, and other agencies of uplift—the moving spirit in this work is the Puerto Rican government's Migrant Division. Much good seems to have been done by these clinics, but the fight is an uphill one. The rent laws and regulations are complex and keep changing all the time, and the Puerto Rican migrants are ill adapted, to say the least, for keeping abreast of them.

New York's low-class housing is often said to be getting poorer and scarcer instead of better and more plentiful. This deterioration is sometimes blamed by the hasty on influxes like that of the Puerto Ricans, but cooler heads say these are only part of the trouble. The latter point out that there was little building in New York during the 'thirties, a depression period, or the 'forties, a period of war and post-war shortages. In the 'fifties there has been a good deal, but little of it is for the poor, if the public housing projects—hardly more than a drop in the bucket—are not counted. Experts say that private builders can't build for the low-income class in New York now, because land costs and construction costs are too high. New building is therefore apt to subtract from the supply of low-class housing, rather than add to it. When a new bridge approach goes in, for instance, a few blocks of slum houses may well be razed to make way for it. When a thoroughfare like Third Avenue is improved, again, other slum housing is razed.

These losses tend to be compensated for by the sinking of middle-class districts into slums—as is happening now in parts of the West Side—while their former inhabitants move off to the suburbs. To some degree the "inner city" tends to go down in value while the suburbs go up. One hears that the same thing is happening in most or all of the big American cities now. In New York's case, however, it is closely linked with the Puerto Ricans' coming, and the latter are apt to be blamed for the whole process, though it is actually hard—perhaps impossible—to separate cause and effect in it.

New York planning experts have made close estimates of the different racial groups in the city, and their tendency to move outside it. These experts conceive of two regions: the city, comprising the five boroughs, and the "environs," comprising seventeen counties round the former. The experts say that in the 'forties the environs increased at two times the rate of the city, but that in the 'fifties the city's increase, if any, has been negligible, while the environs have increased by 50 percent (they are here talking, by the way, of straight numerical increment). In the 'fifties the city has actually been losing its white population, at the rate of about eighty thousand a year (this being subtracted from the 1950 census figure, for whites, of 6,890,000).

The big spurt in the Negro population of New York and its environs took place in the 'forties, when great numbers of them came up from the South, mainly to get war jobs. The Negroes in the city increased by 61 percent in that decade, according to the planners, and those in the environs by 41 percent. In the 'fifties the influx of Negroes to the region has been much less, and their numbers have grown principally through "natural increase," or excess of births over deaths. They have also joined, to some degree, in the suburban drift—in the first half of this decade they have increased by only 12 percent in the city, but by 28 percent in the environs; and they now make up a larger percentage of the population in Westchester than in Queens.

As for the Puerto Ricans, they have been later in coming than the Negroes, of course, and so far they are less suburban in emphasis. In the 'forties the "city" gained thirty-five times as many Puerto Ricans as the "environs" did, and in the 'fifties, so far, it has gained seventeen times as many. This means that the influx of Puerto Ricans is still overwhelmingly an "inner-city" affair, though there are signs that they too are turning suburban.

How this drift goes in the future may depend on economic factors. The planning experts maintain that—if business stays good—the chief growth in manufacturing will henceforth be in the environs, while that in "management activities" will be in the city. This would—if the experts are right—draw numbers of Puerto Ricans and Negroes to the suburbs, where jobs for them would increase; and it would draw more whites to the city, for management jobs, though whether they would live inside it or commute is a question. (Another possibility, somewhat counter to these, should be faced, however—namely that service jobs in the city will increase greatly, and that these will be taken over more and more by Puerto Ricans and Negroes, who will live close in. Among the things that are said to attract Puerto Ricans to New York are the wide variety of jobs here and the tendency of people to rise upward economically in good times, leaving plenty of room at the bottom. This tendency may well increase in the future.)

New York's official planners talk of a population for the city in 1975 of 6,000,000 whites, 1,200,000 Negroes and 1,200,000 Puerto Ricans. This would put the three groups in a 5-1-1 ratio. It should be said that other experts challenge this forecast, maintaining that the white element will be smaller in comparison. And it should further be said that forecasts like this are uncertain, anyway, the events being open to influences that the forecasters cannot reckon on. For instance, at the start of 1950 it looked as if the Puerto Rican migration to New York was tapering off; but then the Korean War broke out, the demand for labor increased here, and the migration was on again as never before.

What unforeseen things may affect it in the future are still, in a word, unforeseen. But certain limits can be made out. For one thing, Puerto Rico's population is only about two million, and even with the wildest increase this source is not enough to swamp New York in the near future. Secondly, unemployment in Puerto Rico is lessening, and the rate of natural increase there is lessening too (partly because so many of the more fertile islanders are in New York). Finally, Puerto Ricans arriving at Idlewild are really beginning to go to the suburbs and hinterland, it seems, rather than staying in the city—the Puerto Rican government's migrant office declares that 35 to 40 percent are now passing on in this way.

For all these reasons, New York can expect that the influx will not get much heavier year by year. But it must also expect it to continue—barring very bad times—and must adapt its public services accordingly. These services have grown vastly since the nineteenth century, it should be noted, and are better able to cope with newcomers than at the time of the big European waves. Also, the city will soon have the help of many bilingual Puerto Rican children now growing up. So absorption should be easier all the time.

The service in New York that has had to change most for the Puerto Ricans, without much doubt, is the school system. In the late 'forties the schools were suddenly flooded with little children who couldn't speak English. The teachers for their part could rarely speak Spanish, and as a result the newcomers were often taught nothing, though they were kept in school anyway, as that was the law, and were also promoted.

"I know Puerto Rican kids in the sixth grade who don't know what two times six are," an athletic coach in the slums told me recently. "So what can they get out of their geography lessons?" Another informant, a slum priest, told me of a Puerto Rican boy who had been in school ten years, but still couldn't read or write, though he had been promoted steadily. Tales like this are common in discussions of the Puerto Rican world here.

In 1957 there were 114,000 Puerto Ricans in New York's public schools, ranging from less than 5 percent of the student bodies in sections like Yorkville and Greenwich Village, to 75 percent or more in sections like East Harlem and the South Bronx. A teacher's job is hardest, I have been told, when Puerto Ricans make up about half of her class, because then they can stay apart from the other children and amuse themselves by talking Spanish—can live their own life, that is, independently of the teaching process that is going on in the same room.

They can get out of hand in these circumstances. "If the Puerto Ricans make up less than 20 percent of a class they get absorbed," a New York school official told me recently. "They will normally learn English fast then, and will go along with the other children. Or if they don't they can at least be disregarded. It is when the Puerto Ricans get to be about 25 to 30 percent of the class that a real problem is created. Then the teacher must control two separate groups, one of which she can hardly communicate with. The problem continues to be bad as you get still more Puerto Ricans—till in the end you lose your English-speakers. Then the teacher's whole time can be devoted to the Puerto Ricans, and her job is simplified again—relatively speaking."

If there are many Puerto Ricans in a school they pose a dual question—how they themselves should be taught, and how the teaching of the English-speakers can be kept up to standard despite their presence. Many English-speaking parents are intolerant of Puerto Ricans, but many, too, are tolerant; the latter don't want the Puerto Rican children neglected in favor of their own; but still they don't want their own to go untaught; and so in the end they often put them in private schools or move to the suburbs.

The schools' problem in all this is made worse by the way Puerto Ricans move about the city, or move to and from their island—Puerto Rican children average a 25 percent turnover during a school year, according to one figure I have been given; and therefore much time is spent, in the classes they attend, on readjustments.

The segregation issue is another thing that complicates the Puerto Rican problem, or limits the schools' freedom to deal with it. From a practical view it might be best to set certain classes, or even certain whole schools, aside for Spanish-speaking pupils, so that they and the English-speaking ones could be given separate, appropriate courses of study. But some of the more articulate Puerto Ricans here are against this solution on principle, arguing that the

Spanish pupils would get the poorer facilities in any such split. The hand of the objectors has been strengthened because the national issue of school segregation is hot now, and in line with this the Board of Education has decreed that all pupils shall be treated the same, as a general rule, regardless of language.

(There are signs, by the way, that a Jim Crow or two-class system *would* develop here if a split in teaching were countenanced. Early in 1957 a settlement-house director named Maxwell Powers charged publicly that an old, dilapidated school in the West Nineties was being used chiefly for Puerto Ricans, whereas a more modern school building near by was being used chiefly for mainland white children. This kind of thing happens often, it seems, when much choice is left to the lower school authorities, who can be open to neighborhood pressures.)

The New York Board of Education has made a survey of Puerto Ricans in its schools, through a special group called the Puerto Rican Study whose staff has numbered up to sixty at times, and which wound up its work in 1957 after nearly four years. The Study's findings have been criticized somewhat, but on the whole they now guide the city's school policy. One item in that policy is that teachers need not know Spanish in order to teach Spanish-speaking children here; indeed, the idea is to get the children out of Spanish and into English as quickly as possible—by the use of pantomime, visual aids, and so forth—and too much talking of Spanish by a teacher is thought to slow this process.

The Study also feels that teaching Puerto Ricans is no longer a job for just a few teachers in a few schools here, but that the whole system must be adapted to it. For this purpose it has gotten out an exhaustive series of pamphlets, aimed at indoctrinating teachers in the things that puzzle Spanish-speaking students—points of English word order, for instance—and at giving them vocabularies of key Spanish words for the better exposition of subjects like science. Most of these pamphlets have been tested in use, and Dr. J. Cayce Morrison, the Study's director, feels that the Puerto Rican school problem will abate steadily now, as the teachers grow familiar with them.

The show school of the city, where Puerto Ricans are concerned, is PS 108, at Madison Avenue and 108th Street, in the heart of El Barrio or Spanish Harlem. Of its fifteen hundred pupils, 94 percent are Puerto Ricans. Cubans, Dominicans, and other Spanish Americans make up 2 percent, and 4 percent are mainland Negroes. English-speaking pupils—or non-Spanish-speaking ones, more strictly— form a tiny minority in the school, therefore, and the teachers can put nearly their whole attention on the Puerto Ricans.

The school follows a variation, apparently, on the general anti-segregation rule—in certain grades it puts newly arrived Puerto Ricans, if they can't speak English well, into "orientation" classes, where much emphasis is laid on their speech; but it gets them out of these and into the "regular stream" as soon as it can. Pupils go only through the sixth grade at PS 108, and after that they move on to a junior high school, where the mainland whites and Negroes are in a much higher proportion. Thus they are broken in to the English-speaking world by stages.

PS 108 also has a kindergarten, and often the children in this can speak no English at all when they arrive. One of the school's three kindergarten teachers is a Puerto Rican herself, and when I visited her class she said she talks Spanish a great deal in the fall—when school has newly opened—in order to put the children at their ease, but switches more and more to English as the year passes. She pointed to one little girl, in a bright red sweater, whose English, she told me, was nearly perfect, though she hadn't known any in the preceding fall, and though her mother still didn't know any and her father knew but little.

The teacher pointed out another child too, a boy, who had come from Puerto Rico only a few weeks earlier. He knew no English at all—so far as she could learn, anyway—and didn't even talk with her in Spanish, though he had begun talking Spanish with the other children after several days of silence. She said this was the usual order of adjustment for kindergarten-age Puerto Ricans—making friends first with fellow pupils, that is, and later with the teacher—though in other cultures the process was often reversed.

PS 108 is a fine brick building, opened in the early 'fifties and well maintained. Mr. Jack August, its principal, told me there had been remarkably little vandalism there—vandalism often being a problem for schools in Puerto Rican and other slums. He said the Puerto Ricans in the neighborhood could be appealed to easily, and were cooperative if given a helping hand. The school, I gathered, was something of an all-around community center, with youth-club activities in the evenings, rent-clinics twice a week, and in the afternoons a service called the All-Day Neighborhood Program, in which psychologically disturbed children, or children whose parents both had jobs, were kept over in the afternoons, fed snacks, and taught things like arts and crafts. It was partly because of these services, I gathered, that the neighborhood had a proprietary feeling about PS 108 and helped to keep it in good shape.

At the school I met a Puerto Rican "S.A.T.," or "substitute auxiliary teacher." There are about seventy of these in the New York school system now, I learned, and they are recruited from Puerto Rico itself. They are not supposed to do actual teaching in New York, because their English accent is thought bad for the purpose—children being such mimics—but they interview new Puerto Rican pupils and show them the ropes, and interview their parents too. They stand by to help the regular teachers if a psychological problem comes up, and they try to speed the adjustment of Puerto Rican pupils' families to New York. The adjustment of all the migrants, in fact, is an objective of the school system.

Not all the city's care is governmental. There are churches, charities, and—above all, perhaps—settlement houses. These last are a special institution, peculiar, it seems, to the English-speaking world, having begun in the slums of London and having been transplanted to New York in 1886, when the University Settlement was founded on the Lower East Side. It has been followed by dozens of others, the most famous of them, perhaps, being the Henry Street Settlement of Lillian Wald, also on the Lower East Side.

The settlement houses have shared the history of New York's immigrant slums. In the first decades of this century they were hard at work among the European masses, trying to help them get better food, better housing, better culture—trying to raise their standards all round, that is. And now in mid-century, with immigration already stopped for thirty years, some of them seem almost to have outlived their usefulness, so well have the standards actually risen in their districts—in parts of the middle East Side, for instance. Other settlement houses, though, have been engulfed by new waves, of Puerto Ricans and of Negroes, and these are busy as never before.

The oldest of them, the University Settlement, has a staff of 120 people and a budget of over $200,000 yearly. Its task is more in the psychological field than it used to be, and less in the economic—the welfare services have, for the most part, taken the latter burden over. The University Settlement now runs, among other things, a mental-health clinic, staffed by a psychiatrist, a psychologist, and a psychiatric social worker. Its fellow settlement houses have the same tendency—to use specialists in psychology—and there is a good demand for these.

Where churches are concerned, the Puerto Ricans are traditionally Catholic, though I have heard it said that 20 percent of those in New York are actively Protestant now. The maker of this statement was not unbiased, and many Catholics would take issue with him. Even if one accepts his figure, though, it is no guide to the amount of aid Puerto Ricans get through officially Protestant channels, for many of the Protestants among them belong to evangelical "store-front" churches, which are not connected with the rich parishes in the city. Yet the gifts of individual Protestants go out to the Puerto Ricans through all kinds of charities—through health funds, camp funds, clothing funds, and so on ad infinitum. The total sum that must change hands this way in New York is staggering to think about, if impossible to measure.

The Catholic position is somewhat different. For one thing the Catholic Church is not a loose assemblage of denominations and parishes—expressing various social backgrounds—but is one big organization for rich and poor alike. And then it does see itself as *the* church of the Puerto

Ricans, even if on their island it has not always tended them closely. In New York it has a definite policy, laid down from above, of assimilating the Puerto Ricans into existing parishes. It also has a centralized service in the so-called Catholic Charities, which does all sorts of things for the migrants.

Finally, of course, there are the Catholic religious orders, whose staffs can be thrown into the struggle. While studying the migrants I have spent some time, off and on, with a member of one of these, a Jesuit father named Walter Janer, who comes of a Puerto Rican family and has grown up partly in New York and partly on the island. Father Janer—the name is pronounced Hahnair, in the Spanish style—is engaged in social work on the Lower East Side. He is attached to Nativity Parish, whose church is on Second Avenue near Third Street. It is a plain, classical Greek Revival building, not looking very Roman Catholic in style; and this can be puzzling till one learns that it was originally built and used by Presbyterians, in the early nineteenth century, when that section was peopled by Scotch-Irish and English. Not long after that the Irish themselves moved in there; the Presbyterians moved out; and the Catholics bought the church building, dedicating it in 1842. A couple of years later it was nearly burned down by an anti-Irish Know-Nothing mob.

Time passed; early in this century Italians began flooding the Lower East Side; and by 1917 they were so numerous there that Nativity Parish was turned over to the Jesuits, who had already done much work among Italian immigrants a few blocks away, on the other side—west, that is—of the Bowery. In 1927 the Jesuits were joined in the parish by some sisters from the Mission Helpers of the Sacred Heart, who established a center a few blocks south of the church, on Forsyth Street, for teaching the catechism and running a day nursery where working Italian mothers could leave their children.

The ground floor and the four floors above it in this structure are now taken up by Father Janer's mission center, where he offers recreation and the like to Puerto Ricans, mainly young ones. The building is small at best, belonging to a row of narrow five-story tenements, which are in different shades of brick and have fire escapes on their façades, along with random touches—in the windows—of laundry and potted plants. They all look across Forsyth Street at a long strip where other tenements have been torn down and where a park and playground now exist, with plane trees and—on warm afternoons—Puerto Rican boys playing stickball. Bowery bums often come to the park too, and sit on the benches, bottle in hand. Normally, I have been told, a patrol wagon shows up at six o'clock and takes them all away, partly because they are deemed a moral hazard to the Puerto Rican and other children after dark.

Father Janer first came to Nativity Parish for six weeks in the summer of 1952, while he was still in training. He had finished his theologate, as it is called, at Weston, Massachusetts, and was about to start on his tertianship—his final year—at Gandía in Spain. The Church had recently grown aware of Puerto Ricans moving into the parish; Father Janer, a Puerto Rican himself, spoke good Spanish; he was also interested in youth and youth movements, and had been studying them, and so he was a natural choice to lead boys'-club work at Nativity that summer.

He did very well at it, by all reports, and the next year he was assigned permanently. Soon afterward three Spanish-speaking American sisters, with long experience in Puerto Rico itself, came to work at the center, and since then Father Janer, on his part, has built up a full-time staff consisting of another Jesuit priest, Father John Hoodack, a Puerto Rican social worker, Luis Colón, and an Irish-American athletic coach, Dan Collins. The sisters attend to the catechistic instruction of the Puerto Ricans round about, and Father Janer and his staff concentrate on social work, especially among the boys.

Father Janer is a medium-sized, wiry young man with glossy black hair and glistening white teeth. He stands straight, though his clothes are often rumpled. He always seems happy. He smiles and laughs a lot, speaks with a New York accent, and expresses himself idiomatically, even slangily, and with Jesuit realism—he has a master's degree in biology, incidentally, and taught physiology and genetics during his latter student years. In the center he is a jack of all trades. Once when I dropped in last winter he was fastening a blackboard to a brick wall, and another time he was fixing a pin-ball machine with a screwdriver.

Each time he greeted me and kept on working. "You'll have to forgive my lack of attention," he said on the second occasion. "These things happen, and you get to be a real handy man. If we had a good budget we'd have people to take care of them, but I think I'd miss it. It's fun to see the kids this way." The kids were playing all round him as he worked, chatting back and forth with him, and I have rarely seen him when he was not liable to interruption of some kind—often by Puerto Ricans with problems.

"One day I am a psychologist, the next a social worker," he remarked to me last winter. "In general I am on the side of youth. We are not trying to hold a torch for delinquents here, but still I do spend a lot of time in the Children's Court on Twenty-second Street, where our Puerto Rican kids keep getting hauled up. I don't try to defend them unduly, of course—justice must be done—but there are often misunderstandings that I can help clarify."

Sometimes Father Janer has been interrupted, when I have been talking with him, by an adult Puerto Rican, in person or on the telephone. "That's a man whose wife's suddenly been hospitalized," he said once, putting the phone down. "He has three small children and no one to care for them. We will have to try and send a volunteer to help him out."

Another time he said, "That woman has a mentally defective boy, and she has been trying to get him into a school that takes such cases. She can't call the school up herself, because she can't speak English. Also, they want the right name, right birth-date, and so forth. She gave them the wrong name a while ago, and that caused trouble. It is all unraveled now, but Father Hoodack and I had to do it. The boy will get into the school all right, as soon as they have room for him. I have told her that too, but she is worried by the delay, and that is why she called up. It is all so mysterious to her."

As for the Puerto Ricans who come to see Father Janer in person, they often arrive with paper forms in hand, which he is supposed to sign as witness or reference. Usually they come by appointment, but often they are late. "Excuse me for a moment," he said to me one day. "There is a woman outside with a paper for me to sign. She was supposed to be here at nine, and now she comes at ten. It happens like that so often. I wish I could change it, but I can't."

He was gone about ten minutes and came back laughing. "I should be like a German," he said. " I should run everything like clockwork, and not waste time on these endless interruptions." But it seemed plain he never would run things that way, and knew it, and was just talking.

Children come to play in the mission center every day after 3 p.m., when school lets out, and Fathers Janer and Hoodack believe that one or both of them should always be on the scene then—partly so they can note if a child stops coming, and can find out why; its parents might be sick, for instance, and might need help. "Above all it's that personal interest," Father Janer says. "You've got to show that you're with them all the way." To this end he visits Puerto Rican families, and hospitals, and walks the streets and talks to the teen-agers there.

The sisters at the center have a house-visiting program too, with a corps of trained lay workers helping in it. The fathers and sisters, between them, run a big program of clubs and discussion groups. There are group discussions on labor and unions for men, on home economics for women, and on religion for adults of both sexes. For the young there are dances, outings, games, and clubs, and a full scouting program run by laymen of the parish.

The center is near a primary school, which lets children out an hour early on Thursdays for "R.T." or "released time," a period intended for religious instruction by the children's own pastors or rabbis. Father Janer told me once that his center would draw over a thousand Puerto Rican children then if it could take them. "Actually we pack in about two hundred," he said. "But even that is too many in the short time—especially as they are so different in age and in their knowledge of English, and are in the mood of just getting out of school. The ideal would be to have four classes of twenty each, but we couldn't possibly hold it down to that."

Father Janer's great work is social work, as noted above, and the religious side is left mainly to the sisters. But he too is mindful of that side, inevitably. "All people," he says, "including young people, are naturally religious, and young Puerto Ricans are naturally Catholic. So I try to make them understand the faith better, of course."

The center has many helpers beyond its immediate staff. A Puerto Rican social worker from Catholic Charities comes for one day a week. He handles "referral" cases—people in need who can be passed on to employers or to the welfare agencies, for instance.

"Or if a child is very disturbed," Father Janer says, "he can refer it to the Catholic Charities' child-guidance clinic. He can refer such cases on with a personal touch. One of the best things he does, really, is to break down that initial fear of going up to a big strange building."

There is also a psychiatric case-worker—a priest who is an old friend of Father Janer's—who comes two evenings a week, mainly to work with problem children. And there are three or four lawyers and doctors who give part-time services free to the center, for legal aid or medical care.

The center has the use of some outside facilities, too, as well as outside personnel—it can, for instance, use a gymnasium at the Holy Name Center on Bleecker Street, and it is entitled to send thirty-two boys away to a camp in the summer, for two weeks each. In these respects it belongs, really, to a greater network of charities and charitable activities in the city. Its own finances are sketchy, for it is a one-horse affair compared to the bigger settlement houses, which have ten times its facilities. It gets a Christmas fund, for toys and other presents, from an annual drive at a Catholic high school in Brooklyn. Part of this money is also used to buy games—little pool tables and the like—for the center itself.

Beyond that, the hat is passed in likely places by Father Janer. "The hardest thing is to beg," he says. "I am learning to do it, but I tell you I hate it." He is also learning to give bingo-and-raffle parties. He gave a big one not long ago at the Statler Hotel, on a Saturday afternoon, which brought in more than four thousand dollars, a slim sum in the face of the center's budgetary needs.

Much of this may actually go toward building a new center, for the whole row of buildings on Forsyth Street is likely to be torn down soon, in favor of a housing project. Father Janer plans ceaselessly for the coming venture, and has hung a sign saying "Pray for the NEW CENTER" inside the present one. It is in blue showcard paint on corrugated cardboard, and has been nicely done by the Father himself—lettering is one of his many accomplishments.

His dreams for the new center include a larger building than the one he has now, with plenty of lounging and reading rooms for boys of different ages, so they can come in off the street, and the little ones can play separately from the big ones, and not be pushed around by them. The Father hopes for a spacious playground too, and possibly for a nursery; and if prayer can get such things he will no doubt have them.

V *The Machine Age*

The Puerto Ricans come to New York because it is their right as citizens. Unlike the European peoples—English, Irish, Germans, Scandinavians, Italians, Jews, and others—who have built the United States up so far, they are not impeded by our immigration laws. They can move to New York about as easily as a Kansas farm boy can, except that they must cross water.

Their special access to the city results, at bottom, from the "American imperialism" of Theodore Roosevelt and his colleagues, who in 1898 led us into the Spanish War and thereby into the seizure of three Spanish colonies: Puerto Rico, Cuba, and the Philippines. These acquisitions were attacked then by some of T. R.'s critics, who argued that the colonies were so unlike our mainland states—in population, language, and culture—that they could never hope to join the Union in the normal way; they would be doomed to second-class dependency, the critics said, which would be without precedent in our history, and dangerous.

The critics failed to carry the day, but have been rather borne out by time. Cuba and the Philippines no longer belong to us, and Puerto Rico has achieved only a half-way, anomalous status, in which her people are citizens but in which she herself is far from statehood—much farther, indeed, than Alaska and Hawaii, which are still waiting. She is the only part of United States territory, furthermore, whose official language is not English (it is Spanish), and this suggests untold problems should she assume a state's relationship with Washington, where words are so important.

She has no true representation in Washington now anyway, in the voting sense, and a few years ago Vito Marcantonio, of New York, used to be called her only congressman. His constituents included the Puerto Ricans of East Harlem, and for their benefit he played the demagogue on Puerto Rican issues—urging the island's independence, for example. The Puerto Ricans of New York, indeed, may well pull more weight in Washington than do the Puerto Ricans of Puerto Rico, and it is a tendency that can grow. So far the migrants do not vote, or register, very heavily, because New York's politics don't mean much to them, but attempts are being made to teach them that voting is a public duty, and they have begun responding to these—nearly a hundred thousand of them registered for the '56 election.

Political leaders of the New York region also—like Mayor Wagner, Governor Harriman, and Governor Meyner of New Jersey—take pains to woo the Puerto Ricans. They don't just woo the migrants, either, but woo their home island as well: Governor Meyner, for instance, made a dramatic visit there on his honeymoon. All this helps give Puerto Rico an indirect voice in American politics.

The Puerto Rican independence movement is not strong on the island now, but it does exist there, and it exists in New York too. In 1956 Governor Muñoz was feted by Freedom House at a dinner in New York's Astor Hotel, and the affair was picketed by migrant *independentistas,* with placards complaining that so notorious a non-believer in freedom—as they saw him—was not qualified for the honor. Again, it was Puerto Rican extremists who shot up Congress a few years ago, and other extremists who tried to shoot President Truman. The Communist Party also exists among the migrants, and it too has independence as a slogan, though it too is quiet now.

"In their hearts my people always yearn for independence," an old Puerto Rican in New York has told me. "They like Governor Muñoz now, because he is transforming the island and making it rich. But in their hearts they want independence, and they will come back to this. They will come back sooner if the island has hard times."

Muñoz's policy—of keeping Puerto Rico in the United States but not seeking statehood—may be the only possible one for him now, but it does underline the island's second-class status and the difficulty of taking it into the States as an equal member. Apparently the Puerto Ricans feel this stress deep down, and New York may feel it too some day, so strong is their voice in the city.

Another assimilation problem—that of the darker Puerto Rican individual—is felt in the migrant world. An outsider cannot easily tell how the color line works in Puerto Rico, but there seems no doubt that dark skin is a worse handicap in New York than there, and that realization of this can shock the dark-skinned migrant.

"For Southern Negroes coming here," I was recently told by a settlement-house psychologist, "discrimination, Northern style, is something they can dope out. But the Puerto Ricans who come haven't had their experience, and for the dark ones especially, it's a new and troubling idea. It is one of the worst bars to their adjustment here, and one of the most disintegrating factors for them emotionally. It is bad for the children especially."

The psychologist paused a moment. "The Puerto Ricans who come here," he went on, "are not suspicious—in the beginning, at least—of advances by whites in other class statuses. With the Negroes you have to pass many more tests. Gambits to Negroes by white work colleagues are relatively easy, but otherwise they are on their guard for a long, long time. The dark Puerto Ricans haven't got these defenses, and they are hurt more easily by the things that happen."

The things that happen to these dark Puerto Ricans include restriction to ghettos, exclusion from good jobs, and social snubs that are less important economically but still hard to take. Virtually all experts on the Puerto Ricans of New York agree that it is hard for the dark ones to move out of their particular slums, like Spanish Harlem, the South Bronx, and the Lower East Side. Fair-skinned Puerto Ricans can move just about anywhere, the experts say, especially if they learn English and grow rich, but the dark ones are left in their ghettos as a residue, like the Negroes.

(The Puerto Rican government, incidentally, discourages its people from moving to our Southern states, where the color line is, of course, still firmer. The government claims to have a laissez-faire policy about the migration, but in truth it influences it a good deal. It doesn't "advise" Puerto Ricans not to go to Dixie, but it "informs them of the conditions" there, which amounts to the same thing. It also refrains from sending contract workers there through its own migrant labor service, though many thousands of these are sent each year to the Northeastern states. Finally, the Puerto Rican government keeps Southern employers from recruiting labor on the island, and from advertising for it there. Again, this is not openly an anti-Southern policy. But employment agencies, or employment schemes, must be approved before they can operate in Puerto Rico, and they are not approved if segregation affects the work they offer.)

When the dark migrants learn about the color line, they

react by differentiating themselves from the Negroes as much as they can. If they go to one of the city's hospitals, for instance, they object if the attendants write them down as "Negro" on the admission forms. Some of them, again, refuse to work on jobs with Negroes. And many of them are loath to learn English. They cling to their Spanish as a badge of distinction, and often they speak it with loud voices in public places, like subway trains. I have heard from various sources that some Negroes in Harlem are learning Spanish too, as a way of ceasing to be Negroes, but I have not been able to verify this.

Another report I have heard is that a relatively small percentage of Puerto Rico's dark inhabitants—as against its light ones—are coming to New York, but this too is hard to verify. If you walk through East Harlem you get the impression that a *large* percentage of dark Puerto Ricans have come up, but then East Harlem is a ghetto, from which the dark ones can escape less easily than the light.

The discovery of our prejudice is said to be especially hard on the "intermediate-colored" Puerto Ricans, such as the so-called *indios* and *grifos,* who have West Indian features or negroid features with fair skin. These types are said to have a somewhat elevated place on the island, above their really dark countrymen, but here they are treated the same. There are other marks of distinction, too, that Puerto Ricans and certain of their Latin American neighbors cling to—and sometimes even fake—but that most mainlanders ignore.

"They have a discrimination of their own," I have been told by a sympathetic union organizer. "You can't treat one who was born in this country like one who wasn't. You can't treat a light-skinned one like a dark-skinned one. And if one was born in Cuba you mustn't call him a Puerto Rican."

So the Puerto Ricans, and Caribbeans, may not have a strong color line, but they do have their little points of caste. And for the higher ones in the scale it is agonizing to be classed with the others.

The New York Negroes are unmoved, on the whole, by these woes of the Puerto Ricans. Many New Yorkers expect solidarity to exist between the Negroes and Puerto Ricans, as they are companions in misfortune, but in fact the reverse is usually true—they are in bitter rivalry for the lowest rungs on the ladder, and the feeling between them is hostile. Some of New York's worst gang wars are between Negroes and Puerto Ricans; and sometimes whites—or "Anglos"—join the Negroes in these. Negro and white boys also "freeze out" the Puerto Ricans, I have been told, in Youth House, the place of detention for young people in Manhattan. Negroes in the housing projects are said to complain often about the Puerto Ricans—about the particular cooking smells they make, for instance. In general, one nearly always hears of friction where Negroes and Puerto Ricans live side by side in the city.

"You have the two groups coming in here," a social worker on the Lower East Side said recently. "They have certain things in common, such as the color problem, and you would expect empathy, but what you really get is rivalry. This is especially true on the teen-age level. You get it in the gangs, and you get it in jealousy of certain facilities, like those of the settlement houses—kids can pretty well control the access to a settlement house, you know, by controlling the street outside. The Negroes were in New York first and had a head start, but now the Puerto Ricans are copying them. They are borrowing the Negroes' gang structure. Also their jive talk or bop language. And their Ivy League stuff in clothing. The white kids are copying them too. The Negroes are setting the pattern, but the Puerto Ricans are right in there contending with them."

A statesmanlike New York Negro told me something, a while ago, about his people's relations with the Puerto Ricans. "Negroes dislike it," he said, "when Puerto Ricans come in and work for less pay. Or when they take an apartment some Negroes have had their eyes on. Puerto Ricans are used again and again to undercut Negroes' wages and pull them down, and naturally that makes for bad feeling. But really the established Puerto Ricans here have the same problem as we do. As soon as they learn English and get to know their rights, the boss wants to get rid of them, and he is out at Idlewild meeting planes. So I tell our people we are all in the same boat. Often, in fact, Puerto Ricans are helpful to Negroes by opening up residential areas to them —they opened up the West Side, for instance, and perhaps also Chelsea and the Lower East Side."

This Negro leader had spent some time in Puerto Rico himself and had taken part in a movement—sponsored by the Puerto Rican migrant office and the Urban League, which does social work among the New York Negroes—to improve understanding between the two groups. He plainly believed in the principle of united we stand, divided we fall—believed, that is, that the Negroes couldn't indulge in prejudice against the Puerto Ricans if they were going to fight prejudice against themselves.

A great many other persons and institutions in New York believe the same thing. They include churches, unions, city departments, social services, and the personnel of these, and they are trying their best to end the Negroes' and Puerto Ricans' strife. So far, one gathers, they are doing all right on the high level of talk, but less well on the lower one of actual getting together.

One key meeting place of Negroes and Puerto Ricans is in the field of music—the meeting of the jazz and Latin rhythms that mean so much to the respective cultures. These seem to be coming together somewhat and affecting each other—one can hear the results, for instance, at the Palladium Ballroom. But the two groups are still far from any real cultural fusion. "Each thinks the other is a little square," as one man put it to me after attending a musical get-together of theirs.

The two groups aren't close, really, but are on sufferance with each other. This is all right now, the experts seem to think, and may get better—unless, that is, we have a bad slump. If we have that, with bad unemployment, the experts say, real trouble between the Negroes and Puerto Ricans can be expected. Or trouble among the Puerto Ricans themselves, for that matter.

The Puerto Rican disharmonies in New York have a deep background in history, and they can be understood better if one considers this. Migrations have gone on since prehistoric times, of course, by land and sea, though this is the first really airborne human one. Some migrations have been economic—away from hunger—and some ideological—away from persecution. This one is in the former class and thus seems less noble, in a way, than some in the latter—the movements of the Jews, for instance, or of the Christian colonists to North America. It also seems less sweeping, or historically significant, than others in its own, economic, class—than that, say, of the millions of Chinese to Southeast Asia, or of the classical Indo-European waves to the Mediterranean.

Historically, it is a straight result of the Renaissance and of the Western outrush that followed. That outrush was led by the Iberian countries, Portugal and Spain, who were among the first to gain from the Renaissance's new spirit and techniques of seafaring. Later the more northern seaboard countries, like Holland, France, and England, took the movement up. Between them the Europeans seized much of Asia, Africa, and the Americas, subduing or displacing the people there, and sometimes transporting them in slavery. The aims and motives of the outrush were variously explained by its participants, but one theme—the altruistic—recurred again and again in their arguments, whether sincerely or otherwise. The Asians, Africans, and primitive Americans, it was said, were being saved from themselves—they were being given Christianity and its benefits, and in the end they would be civilized, or raised to the Western standard.

Later a sub-development took place within the outrush. Its early leaders—Spain especially, perhaps—grew tired, and certain Spanish colonies came to be looked on by other parts of Christendom—notably the United States, with its North European settlers—as back in the original condition, more or less: as dark and unredeemed, that is, and still in line for saving. With this thought in mind, we Yankees took California and part of our Southwest from Spain in 1846, in the Mexican War, and we took Puerto Rico in 1898, in the Spanish War, as already noted. Like the earlier seizures, these, and especially that of Puerto Rico, were accompanied by vows of altruism—of intent to civilize the people and raise them to the Western standard, or rather, this time, to the United States one.

Thus the Puerto Ricans have twice had the promise of being raised up, and if justice were mathematical they might claim to belong doubly in the ranks of those Asians,

Africans, and Americans who are now beating on the door of their onetime conquerors, demanding entry to the club as equals. These ranks include such scattered groups as the Asians and Africans still under colonial rule; the American Negroes, seeking integration; and several newly free peoples, like the Indians, who are clamoring for an equal voice in running the world through bodies like the United Nations.

How to deal with all these groups, in view of the past promises, is one of the hardest questions now facing the Western world. Different answers to it are being worked out in many far-flung places. But where the Puerto Ricans are concerned, an answer is being worked out right in New York, through the day-to-day job of assimilating them.

New York's historical role in the outrush, a peculiar one, also bears on the Puerto Rican question. In some places the outrushing Europeans mixed with the natives—as in certain Portuguese colonies and Puerto Rico, too (though in Puerto Rico's case a third strain, the African, was added). In other places the Europeans merely subdued the natives and ruled over them, without mixing greatly—as the British did in India, for instance. And in still others they eliminated the natives, also without mixing—by wiping them out or confining them to remote spots in the hinterland. It was the third of these fates that befell North America—above the Rio Grande, anyway—and so United States history descends mainly from European history, without much of a native contribution.

At first the Europeans landed everywhere on the Atlantic Coast—Plymouth Rock, Jamestown, St. Augustine, and so forth—but in the nineteenth century they converged more and more on New York, which turned into a sort of funnel for receiving them. They came in greater and greater volume, and New York became able to take a million of them yearly. It developed a way of sucking them in at the bottom, economically, and working them upward, or outward to the hinterland. It processed them, that is, and their labor helped it grow.

Then the flow was checked, in the nineteen twenties, by immigration laws. It was not missed at first, apparently—lots of raw immigrants were in New York already when it stopped, awaiting absorption, and then came the depression and the abnormality of war. But with peace and good times, in the late 'forties, it began to look once more as if New York life was really predicated on a supply of cheap new labor—to do the jobs the older immigrants wouldn't do—and at that stage the Puerto Ricans rushed in to help.

One fruit of the heavy immigration years was the "Americanization process." A Puerto Rican friend who came up in the 'twenties as a small boy recently gave me his views on this, and they were not tender.

"How do you become an American?" he asked. "Why, you give up your background and language. You are changing from one culture to another, and the price you pay is to become colorless."

He told me that he had been raised in his early years on a Long Island farm, by an Anglo-Saxon Protestant family with whom his father had left him because he—the father—had had no home of his own then. Later he had remarried, though, and had brought my friend, still a small boy, to live in a cold-water flat in East Harlem.

"I'll never forget the first time I stood on the stoop there," my friend told me. "I knew only two words of Spanish when I crossed the East River, and I was much more of an American, culturally, than the immigrant boys around me in the street. I stood there and watched the young men and teen-agers playing. Some were playing stickball and some were throwing dice—things I had never seen and didn't under-stand. Later I saw boys stealing potatoes from the horse-drawn wagons that went by. They would put them in tin cans and cook them over fires in empty lots—making mick-eys, they called it. I learned to make them too, and they were very nourishing.

"I learned fast in those days. I remember a freckle-faced boy coming up to me and saying, 'Hey you, what are you?' 'I'm an American,' I said. 'Yeh, yeh, I know that,' he an-swered, 'but what *are* you?' Finally it came out that I was a Puerto Rican. 'Oh, so you're a spik?' he said, and then we had to fight. Everybody was spiks and wops and micks and kikes in those days. A kid would have this pounded into him, and he would try to hide his nationality and be like everyone else. An Italian kid would be ridiculed as a spaghetti-bender, and he would get ashamed and turn away from his parents."

Today it was the same with the Puerto Rican children, my friend went on. "In school the teacher will say, 'Don't speak Spanish.' She really means 'Speak more English,' but she puts it in that negative way and the kids feel ashamed. Or a nutritionist will say, 'Tell your mother not to give you rice and beans.' She really means, 'Tell her to give you other things too,' but the way it is put sounds like criticism, and the kids get the idea their parents are in the wrong. And then they keep hearing all the city's ills blamed on the parents—you know how the talk against Puerto Ricans goes here. So of course they reject them. Or else they retreat into their own group."

My friend warned against trying to assimilate the Puerto

Ricans too quickly in New York. "If you say 'Don't read a Spanish paper,' they won't read any paper," he said. "And if you say 'Don't join a Spanish-speaking group,' they won't join any group. So it is better to get them adjusted within the Puerto Rican community, and not try to make them leave it entirely."

My friend has given much thought to this subject, yet one wonders. One sees so many second-generation immigrants now who have lost their old nationality—all trace of it—that one cannot but hold the Americanization process in awe. The Jewish communities in New York have been reputed somewhat immune to it, because of their strong religion and culture, but even this immunity is threatened now, one hears, by the Jewish migration to the suburbs. Dr. Oscar Handlin, for instance, the authority on immigration, points out that suburban life—where everyone's role is cut out for him, more or less, and where each man knows his neighbor's business—will expose the Jews much more to the cultural leveling of Americanization.

And it may be, one feels, that Americanization, suburban life, mass production, and our famous United States trait of conformity—even McCarthyism too—are all related. America is a big country, made up of diverse elements. Perhaps a fine-grinding process has been inevitable. Anyway, as my friend has pointed out, the Puerto Ricans are being ground a bit now in New York, which can be called the great immigration-mill of all time.

Many efforts are being made, on the world-wide scale, to fulfill the old promises about raising up non-Western peoples. One line they take is economic, and there they express themselves in the "Point Four" approach, which aims at imbuing the non-Westerners with our skills, techniques, and machines. Most of this work is done in the faraway lands themselves, but it can be done within the West if representatives of the faraway peoples are brought here—as they are, for instance, in many Point Four training programs.

The assimilation of the Puerto Ricans in New York, as laborers, can be looked on as part of this effort, too. (Historically, Puerto Rico should be counted as part of the West, without much doubt; but from the Point Four view it—like many other parts of Latin America—can be seen as really non-Western, in that until recently it had a primitive, peasant economy little affected by industrialism.) To the migrants, their work in New York is mainly a living, of course, but in a larger view it is a process that transforms them—as would a training program—and through them helps transform their whole people.

Some lines of Puerto Rican work in New York go back several decades. Puerto Ricans were in cigar-making here quite early in this century, for instance, and prospering at it, since that industry—from which Samuel Gompers came— was the fountainhead, so to speak, of our labor movement. A Puerto Rican cigar maker who came here in 1921 has told me that he and his colleagues made thirty-five to forty dollars a week in those days.

Other Puerto Ricans have been less fortunate. The corrugated-box industry in New York is also an old Puerto Rican stamping-ground, and a man who came up to join it in 1930 has told me that a few years later, in the deep depression, it was paying only six or eight dollars a week, thanks largely to the supply of new, green Puerto Ricans coming in on the boats which the factory owners would go down regularly to meet. Since then things have changed, however—the industry has been unionized and considerably mechanized, and a job there is a different kind of thing now.

Not long ago my friend who had come up in 1930—he is still connected with the industry—took me out to see a corrugated-box plant in Queens. There are many such plants in and around New York, it seems, and he told me this one was of average size. It was housed in a newish brick building with a huge expanse of concrete floor, bigger than a football field. The air in it was full of hums, roars, throbbings, bangs, and clickings, plus an assortment of chemical smells, among them that of printer's ink.

Towering stacks of corrugated cardboard sheets stood round, and so did dollies with smaller stacks of sheets, and many big rolls of plain brown paper. Some of these rolls were being carried about by fork lifts, and one was being installed in a big machine—scores of yards long—that looked like a rotary newspaper press. This was called a combiner, my friend said. The paper ran through it in long strips, some of it being corrugated on the way and all of it being pasted together to make the board that we know in cartons. Afterward the board was taken away to other machines, which could cut it to various sizes and score it for folding.

The combiner was the key piece of equipment, my friend explained, since it turned out raw material for the others. It had many different adjustments on it, to be set and watched, and it was fed and supervised by half a dozen men, the chief of whom was called the operator and drew a weekly base pay of eighty-three dollars, which meant a take-home pay of considerably more. This particular operator was a Puerto Rican, and so were some of those assisting him—threefourths of the men in the whole plant were Spanish-speaking, my friend told me, which meant that they were Puerto Ricans, by and large.

We walked round and looked at other machines—dozens of them—which were cutting board, creasing it, or printing legends on it—sometimes printing complex jobs in several colors. Most of them seemed advanced in design and exacting to run, but without much hard labor involved in them. "See how easy it is today," my friend would say as we paused at one. "Years ago we used to break our backs." Or he would say, "Years ago it was a different machine altogether. We used to work like a dog." He pointed out heavy loads being carried round the plant mechanically, by fork lifts and other means, and said such things had all been done by hand in the 'thirties—it had taken two men to put a roll of paper in the combiner, for instance. In the 'thirties too, as he had told me, some workers in corrugated plants had earned only six or eight dollars weekly, but now those in this plant earned a minimum of sixty-four, with some getting more than twice that.

About that time I also visited a foam-rubber plant and an aquarium supply house. The latter was in the Bronx and had numbers of workmen, among whom were many Puerto Ricans, busily assembling the little gadgets like aquarium-heating elements that tropical fish in New York seem to need. One of the place's owners told me that the only drawback to Puerto Rican labor was the language problem.

"There are half a dozen people on this floor," he said, "that I can't really talk to. If I want to tell them something—especially about a new operation—I must do it through the foreman, and I'm not sure he is putting it just the way I'd like to. Also those who don't know English can't read the signs and notes on our bulletin board here, which are not vital, but which do help a worker keep in better touch with the business."

Apart from the language question this employer had no

fault to find with the Puerto Ricans, who he said worked as well as anyone. "There's no discrimination here," he added. "We're Jewish ourselves, and we've experienced that, and we're against it."

The foam-rubber plant was on the Upper West Side of Manhattan. It didn't manufacture foam rubber, but cut it up and reshaped it for buyers in New York. Its raw material —foam rubber or sometimes synthetics like it—came to the place in thick airy slabs, perhaps in the natural off-white of latex, or perhaps dyed in pastel tones or more lurid colors. The workmen handled it, rolled it, cut it into sheets and shapes, put bevels and curves in it, and finally pasted it together into new shapes with rubber cement.

"All these curves and fancy shapes must be just so with modern furniture," I was told by my guide, a union organizer. "A woman dreams of a chair with a certain curve to it, and it must be that way."

The men catering to these demanding tastes included many Puerto Ricans, and I learned from a foreman that in this plant, again, the Puerto Ricans' main difficulty was with language. Weakness in English could prevent them from advancing into really skilled jobs, for in these they would have to follow orders that came in on paper, as blueprints or as notes with dimensions written in.

I watched one Puerto Rican cutting a bevel in a block of foam rubber, working from notes and figures scribbled on a large sheet of brown paper. I couldn't understand these myself, but they seemed clear enough to him. He spoke English with hardly an accent, incidentally, and on my asking he said he had studied the language a good deal, on his own, and had practiced by reading the newspapers. He had been on this job seven years, he told me, and had been a carpenter before that—"cutting wood and cutting foam rubber are pretty much the same," he said, though I don't know how seriously he meant this.

The Puerto Rican government's Migrant Division has had much experience, too, with language as an impediment to its clients. One day when I was in the Migrant Division I was told, more or less at random, of two men who had been set back by language. One was a grocer—the keeper of a Spanish-American *bodega*—who had been here since the 'thirties; he had recently lost his store, apparently, and had turned to the Migrant Division for help in finding a job; but he had never learned much English, and his choice was limited as a result. The other man had been making forty dollars weekly in Puerto Rico, as a cook in a good hotel there; then he had come to New York, but as he knew little English the best job he could get was a dishwashing one, which was distinctly a comedown.

The Migrant Division deals with a huge number of laborers. In 1956 it interviewd thirty thousand of them about jobs alone, and it interviewed many more about other things, such as unfair treatment they had had from employers. The office is able to fill most of the demands for labor made on it, I have been told; but one that it can't quite keep up with is the demand for skilled sewing-machine operators in the garment trade. When I checked with the office some time ago, I found that one New York garment manufacturer was training his own Puerto Rican operators then—mostly women—so badly did he need them.

The Puerto Ricans are rated pretty good union members by their colleagues in New York, though they are sometimes easily intimidated because of their ignorance. Being at the bottom of the labor class structure, too, they are often preyed on by racketeering unions. Where legitimate unions are concerned, they are most apt to be found in those with a CIO background —since those with AFL backgrounds tend more toward exclusiveness or monopoly by the old-time workers. In general, Puerto Ricans are pretty well out of the waterfront, carpenters', painters', bricklayers', and teamsters' unions. They are pretty well entrenched in the various garment-trade and hotel-and-eating-place unions, and in miscellaneous unions having to do with light manufacturing and the service trades.

Some unions, or at least their New York locals, are flat out against discrimination of any sort now, partly in reaction to Hitler's racist theories, which shocked their members in the 'thirties and 'forties. This anti-discrimination tendency is shared by, among others, the ILGWU, the Hotel Workers' Union, and District 65 of the Retail, Wholesale, and Departmental Store Union, an omnium-gatherum that includes many light-manufacturing, as well as department-store, workers.

The anti-discrimination policy is a boon to the Puerto Ricans, because the unions that follow it may use their hiring halls to make employers take Spanish-speaking workers willy-nilly. District 65, for instance, has thus forced certain corrugated-box plants to hire Puerto Ricans though some of them are loath to do so nowadays, when minimum-wage rules make the exploitation of foreigners no longer profitable. "Sometimes a boss says he can't use workers who don't speak good English," a District 65 official told me recently. "We answer that he could use them all right when he paid them only eight dollars a week, so he's going to use them now too."

Union control of a shop's choice of workers, through hiring halls, has sometimes also been used to break up a sort of reverse segregation that has existed in New York.

Some small shops here have had all Puerto Rican or all Negro labor in the past, with those groups tending to guard
their hold on them jealously. But recently the unions have
been forcing mixed crews on such shops. This increases the
union's power over the industries they deal with, and incidentally it adds to New York's effectiveness as a leveler, or
a producer, of sameness.

A bit more can be learned about the Puerto Ricans as
workers, perhaps, by a comparison between them and the
Mexicans who come in through our Southwest and who
make up our other big source of Hispanic labor. The two influxes actually meet, it happens, at Chicago. The Puerto
Ricans, flying in via Idlewild, fan out that far, and the Mexicans have been coming there for many years—doing cheap
labor there and camping in freight cars. The Puerto Ricans
make out a good deal better than the Mexicans in Chicago,
I have been told by a man who knows both groups there.
This is partly because they are citizens, he says, and partly
because the Mexicans have a long tradition in the city of
discrimination and underprivilege, which the Puerto Ricans
don't share.

Another informant, who has observed the Puerto Ricans
here and the Mexicans in the Southwest, told me recently
that the latter are more primitive by our standards. "The
Mexican culture at home has never felt the impact of our
own," he said, "as the Puerto Rican has since 1898. Perhaps
as a result the Puerto Ricans are relatively aggressive, in a
good sense. They feel they are pioneers when they come to
New York, and they look eagerly to whatever is new. They
are willing to work well and hard. They have real manual
dexterity, as they show in the garment industry and in as-

sembling TV and radio sets. The Mexicans don't get into things like that, though. They are much more tied to a pre-industrial culture—they have more identity with older folkways."

This man told me about a study, made recently, of the objects in a number of Mexican and Spanish houses in the Southwestern states. "Quite different kinds of artifacts were found in them side by side," he said. "Some were of modern design, some were of Spanish-colonial design, and some even of pre-Columbian—30 per cent, in fact, were pre-Columbian. Of course you would find almost nothing of pre-Columbian design in a Puerto Rican dwelling here, or even on the island. Most of the things would be modern. All in all, I think it is fair to say that the Puerto Ricans have come much farther into modern times than the Mexicans."

This man warned me that his views were not "scientific" —were merely "untested assumptions"—but still they seemed to throw some light on the situation. It should be remembered, though, that the Puerto Ricans come to the most highly industrial part of the States, whereas the Mexicans come to an agricultural part, in California and the Southwest, and come for agricultural jobs almot exclusively. The different aspirations of the two groups—as well as their different backgrounds—may easily affect their outlooks.

The Puerto Ricans' capacity for further advance into modernism is something I have heard different views on. In labor circles I have heard that they are often not ambitious on a job, and will refuse promotion to some higher stratum—to the operation of a more complex machine, for instance—because the pay there is only a dollar more a week, say, and they are happy where they are. I have also heard that many gifted Puerto Rican youths drop out of the educational system in New York between junior and senior high school because they don't know their own potentiality —they can't visualize how much higher they may climb in the end if they keep up their schooling.

Finally, I have heard that most immigrants to the United States—from Germany, Ireland, or wherever—have generally stuck at first to the class from which they came in the old country—middle-class ones have joined the middle-class, that is, and laborers have joined the laboring class. To the extent that this is true, it should inhibit the Puerto Ricans a good deal, as so many of the ones who migrate come from the lowest class in a heretofore static, peasant society.

Yet on the other hand I have been told, by a man who has a small but high-grade lamp-assembly shop in New York, that the Puerto Ricans are the only laborers in town now who want to do an honest day's work, and that the vocational training they get in their island high schools—if they go to these—is better than what they would get on the mainland. So their potentiality for rising should not be minimized.

The intensity of English-teaching—so important to assimilation—has varied in the past on the island, so that Puerto Ricans of different ages speak it with different degrees of skill. "People in their late thirties and upward are apt to speak good English," I have been told by a mainlander in San Juan. "Then down to their early twenties they are apt to speak it poorly. But below that they are apt to speak it well again, because English-teaching in the schools was stepped up a few years ago. Then again, city people are apt to speak it well, and country people are apt not to." As city people are on the wax in Puerto Rico now, and as the schools are getting steadily better under the Muñoz regime, it may be that English will bloom more and more.

Another hopeful fact is that Professor I. A. Richards, one of the developers of Basic English, has been working on the Puerto Ricans' language problem in New York. He and some associates, in co-operation with the Hudson Guild, a big settlement house in Chelsea, have been teaching English to Puerto Ricans through animated pictures on a closed TV circuit. Some time ago, Richards said that the program had already given a new confidence to many Puerto Ricans and had been taking one or two hundred of them off the relief rolls each month, by helping them qualify for jobs. Since the Richards method of teaching language, by pictures, is a supposedly universal one, worked out thoughtfully over several years, it may well be found useful for Puerto Rico itself in time.

Finally, the development of the island's own economy must affect the capacity of all Puerto Ricans to change and adapt. Under Operation Bootstrap the island itself is perhaps changing as much now as any region on earth. It is getting industry at a great rate, and its agriculture is being mechanized—thirty thousand workers have left agriculture in the past five years, I was recently told in Puerto Rico, but production has stayed the same despite this. Home needlework, a great thing in the island's tradition, has also been diminishing—in the face of competition from Japan and the Philippines—and some of the labor thus released has been going into the new light industry there.

On visiting Puerto Rico one repeatedly gets the impression that the way of life is in flux. At the airport of San Juan a porter placed my typewriter (a large, squarish portable) upside down when moving it, and I have learned in Asia to take this as a sign of primitiveness—a sign that the porter doesn't recognize the typewriter but assumes it is a box, with the shallow part of the container as its lid. On the other hand, I saw workmen cleaning the airport's waiting-room floor with a big tractor-like machine, instead of with mops, and that seemed a distinct sign of mechanization.

One man in Puerto Rico told me that the islanders can, because of their temperament, stand repetitive work at machines much better than we mainlanders can. Another told me that they learned "semi-skilled manipulative opera-tions"—the running of machines—more easily than main-landers because they were more malleable, thanks to their lack of a factory tradition; their limbs were not grooved, he meant, in old habitual motions as a Yankee operator's might be. This man added that the same lack of a factory tradition worked against the Puerto Ricans, though, in the development of high-grade technicians, such as engineers.

Still another man told me that the Puerto Rican govern-ment was accompanying Operation Bootstrap by a small side effort called Operation Serenidad—a study aimed at learning how Puerto Ricans could industrialize without the nervous wear and tear that usually goes with that process. Yet that such a study might be superfluous was suggested by another thing I heard: namely, that the minimum wage in the island's garment industry had recently been raised, and that as a result many Puerto Ricans had stopped work-ing a full week, on the grounds that they could afford this and would do better to take it easy.

All in all, I got the impression in Puerto Rico of a carefree tropical people being mechanized at a fast clip and adap-ting well enough. I also got the idea of social transforma-tion. "There is a rising middle class in Puerto Rico," as one man told me. "It is neither peasant nor proletarian. It in-cludes such people as social workers, minor industrialists, and the like. Through this class, more and more Puerto Ricans are getting what they want right on the island itself. Those in the new class, and those related to it, are a stabilizing force, and this will be felt both on the island and among the migrants in New York."

Puerto Rico has an inside track, so to speak, in the Point Four race that has been going on of late. Among all the world's "economically underdeveloped" regions, it is perhaps the one that is being redeemed the most quickly, because of its tie with the United States mainland. It is conscious of this, and it repeatedly offers itself as a training ground and laboratory for the general Point Four advance—as a bridge, in other words, by which American techniques can spread to still less developed places. The University of Puerto Rico, at Rio Piedras, is now serving as a nucleus for Point Four teaching and discussion, with aspiring technicians coming to it from all over—mainly from Latin America, but also from Asia and Africa. An atomic study center for Latin Americans has been established there too. The Catholic University at Ponce, on its part, has another ambitious program for transmitting United States knowledge to Latin Americans. The fine Puerto Rican vocational schools have also played host to thousands of Latin American students, and, finally, a steady stream of foreign Point Four workers passes through the island on look-see trips. All this gives a sense of higher purpose to Puerto Rico's transformation, which must be an added inspiration to the men who are leading it.

"Point Four" is a vague idea. In a way it just means modernization. Or it means enshrining the "Protestant ethic" in lands heretofore without it—enshrining the values of

Poor Richard's Almanac, one might say. Again, it means trying to raise faraway peoples to the Western standard economically. It is in direct line of succession to the old American missionary effort—to both the religious and secular
aspects of this, the latter including things like medical and
educational missionary work. The phrase "Point Four" has
been used far and wide to denote the miscellaneous kinds
of advancement that Puerto Rico, for one, has been experi-
encing.

In the larger, historical view, this advancement is part
fulfillment of the old promises. Another part fulfillment of
them is our attempt at binding Puerto Rico into the United
States politically. Still a third is our attempt—however difficult—at transcending the color line on our mainland. And
a fourth is New York's performance as an immigration-mill
for the Puerto Ricans. All these activities seek to redeem our
promise of "One World."

Some side discoveries are made when one explores this
question of union and adaptation, via the Puerto Ricans and
New York. One of these is what might be called the texture
of the American community. Time and again, when asking
experts about the Puerto Ricans in New York, I have met
the complaint that they lack leadership, or lack organizations of their own. It has then come out that this is a necessity in American life now—especially, perhaps, in big cities.

Recently a social worker was telling me about his approach to the Puerto Ricans. "We visit them in the housing
projects," he said, "and draw them into activities. They must
have a way to express themselves, and we want to develop
initiative in their community itself, so they can make a contribution. This initiative unfolds through settlement-house
programs, P.T.A.-type activities, and so forth. The Puerto
Rican leaders have to rise through their own circles before

they can function in the community leadership. So we feel we must get them in action—in action together as Puerto Ricans, and then also in action with others."

At first I couldn't understand the need for all this stirring-up. But later some Health Department people told me that it was hard to reach individual Puerto Ricans here because they hadn't developed community groups through which this could be done. And other city officials told me that no minority group had grown strong in New York until it had raised up its own leaders. So finally it dawned on me that most individuals can't find a true position in society here nowadays—can't "relate," as the social worker might have put it—unless they are held in place by a tissue of clubs, unions, and other groupings.

The Puerto Ricans, it seems, are not "joiners" by tradition, and so they have a hard time fitting into this pattern of ours. On their island their family and village relationships are enough to give them a sense of "belonging," but in New York these aren't enough. Something else must be found, and that is one of the hardest parts of their adjustment. (I have been assured that the problem will solve itself, however, when New York's present Puerto Rican children grow up, as they are being fully indoctrinated—by the schools, settlement houses, boys' clubs, Scouts, and so forth—in the "joining" idea.)

Another discovery one makes is that huge migrations take place within the forty-eight states. A knowledgeable Puerto Rican has told me that five million Americans move from one state to another each year. More of this movement is toward big cities than away from them, and I have read that such trends exist in other countries too, including the Communist ones, and that they are blamed for a general decline in urban law and order—it is widely said that when country people move to the city they lose their old virtues without at once finding new ones. New York is far from unique in having trouble with its newcomers.

A third discovery, or reminder, that one gets in the Puerto Rican quest concerns our immigration laws—one is reminded, in brief, that these seem to have been drafted with almost no eye on the realities. The laws are based on an apparently false assumption—namely, that we do not need a continuing influx of raw labor in this country. So they cut off the traditional sources of such labor; but since it is really needed anyway, it is obtained from new sources, with much more limit on the choice. Puerto Ricans may or may not make the best possible addition to New York's labor pool, but the city must take them anyway because the immigration laws, in effect, decree as much.

And then a fourth discovery is that many people dealing with the Puerto Ricans here—like city officials and social workers—lean so far backward to avoid prejudice that they resist seeing any difference between the migrants and the mainlanders. They seem to take it on faith that all men are not only equal, but the same. This attitude has a deep background in American beliefs, and owes much as well to the reaction against Hitlerism—certainly the tendency to differentiate between peoples has lessened greatly in New York in the past two or three decades. This is no doubt a gain for tolerance, but it seems also to be slight loss for realism. Puerto Ricans *are* different from native New Yorkers in some respects.

It might be said, in passing, that trying to make Puerto Rico like our mainland, through Point Four and similar methods, is not the only promising avenue toward One

World. Encouraging it to be opposite from us, or complementary, has good points too.

When I was on the island I found this confirmed in a couple of ways. One was in the tourist business. I stayed near the Caribe Hilton Hotel when in Puerto Rico, and I went there often. It is a tall modernistic slab of a building, and hundreds of New Yorkers were living in it, enjoying a view, from their windows, out over the strange blue tropical sea. On coming downstairs these guests could stroll through breeze-drenched lobbies with aviaries dotted here and there—with flamingoes wading in pools by the elevators, for instance. They could sit in armchairs at a knee-high bar while sunken bartenders mixed them exotic drinks—served up, perhaps, in coconut shells with straws.

It all seemed very restful, and its main virtue, so far as I could tell, was its difference from New York. I gathered that Puerto Rico's hotel space for first-class tourists—already in four figures—was being sorely taxed at the time and would soon be doubled, which would mean, I felt sure, bigger earnings for the island and real fun for more mainlanders as well.

On that trip I also visited a nursery, known as Pennock's Gardens, that raises tropical plants for the New York market. Mr. Charles Pennock, the owner, told me that he competed with Florida and Texas nurseries in the case of some plants, including philodendron, but that Puerto Rico had other plants to itself through enjoying a perfect climate for them the year round. Mr. Pennock's son took me through the nursery and showed me huge expanses of young philodendrons growing in the shade of green plastic screening. They looked like expanses of young beans. And he showed me tables covered with other philodendrons, being packed for air shipment by Puerto Rican women. He told me that one or two thousand plants left the nursery for Idlewild each week, and that business was booming at the moment.

"As the standard of living goes up in the States," he said, "it seems that more and more plants are needed there." This must be a good thing for Puerto Rico, I felt; and it is good for New York, too, that the island can decorate our homes so.

The Puerto Ricans don't all take kindly to their Americanization, whether it occurs on the mainland or their island. Often they react in some form of anti-Americanism, as people in so many countries are doing now, when faced by Americanization or the machine age or both—the two must seem much the same to viewers in many places, as they come from the same direction.

Often the Puerto Ricans react, it seems, by a withdrawal into Latinism, and a tendency to glorify Spanish culture. One authority has told me that there used to be three cultures in Puerto Rico before 1898—the Indian, the Spanish, and the Negro—but that these have since fused in opposition to the American. An educated Puerto Rican woman in New York recently bewailed a loss of emotional feeling that she said her people suffered from because of Americanization. She told of unspoiled Puerto Rican women "who leave their job and everything else to go see their mother, and then they have lived emotionally." She said New York opposed tendencies like this, and she regretted having lost them somewhat herself through living here.

Anti-Americanism is also expressed in the songs Puerto Ricans sing here. Some of these, with running summaries in English, can be found on the record called *Nueva York*, assembled by Tony Schwartz and published by Folkways Records. One of them says, in part: ". . . And with the English language I am always mixed up. . . . Whenever I have to take an elevator I start trembling from head to foot. . . . I am going back to Puerto Rico even if I have to go back swimming. There even just eating bananas I will go through life singing."

Another one of the songs says, also in part: "I am going back to my little island. There I was much better. . . . Here all the bad customs have come to me. When I go to a dance if somebody tells me something I want to fight. . . . I got contagious since I came to New York. I am going back to my country. There I was very much better."

These songs seem typical of all the laments made throughout history for a Golden Age, or an innocence that is lost—and can seldom be regained, alas, even by going back swimming. Many of us mainlanders would agree with the singers, undoubtedly, as we contemplate modern life. In this sense anti-Americanism can be called an American trait, as well as a foreign one.

Further confirmation of that fact may be found in the way some New Yorkers seem to be withdrawing into Latinism now along with the Puerto Ricans. The study of Spanish is booming in the city, and so is the attempt to learn Caribbean dance steps. A visit to the Palladium Ballroom on a Wednesday evening will discover scores of Yankees taking mass instruction there—and silently and stiffly, like rheumatic ghosts, trying to make the motions that Puerto Ricans make so naturally. There is nothing new about this sort of cultural exchange. Rome organized the peoples round about her, and in return they infiltrated her with their anti-Roman ways. It is part of the eternal creation of One World.

And in the present case—the modernizing of Puerto Rico —the work may really go well, for the Christian Spaniards

helped prepare the way. The Philippines, another old Spanish colony, are far less anti-American now than are the
nearby parts of Asia. The Filipinos like our gadgets, our
clothes, our huckstering, and our way of doing things. And
on the whole, really, the Puerto Ricans like them too, and
no doubt for the same reason—that in recent centuries their
culture has been fairly close to ours, despite the obvious
differences.

VI *El Barrio Revisited*

I ceased my more diligent phase of studying the Puerto Ricans in June of 1957, when the summer heat was on. Then I left New York awhile, and when I came back I was busy with other things and did not hurry to revisit them. And as the weeks passed they grew dim to me, as they easily can to New Yorkers. I knew they were there, but they weren't in the foreground of my thoughts.

Then in October I learned that on Columbus Day, New York's Spanish community would lay wreaths at the Columbus statue in Central Park. This ceremony would be distinct from the regular Columbus Day parade, I gathered, and would play up the discoverer's link with Spain as opposed to his Genoese origin (for Columbus Day has become a quasi-Italian festival in New York since the immigrants came from that country). The day happened to fall on a Saturday, and it dawned bright and clear, so I decided it might be a good time for a reunion.

I went first, at about 3:30 p.m., to the corner of Fifth Avenue and Fifty-ninth Street—the square in front of the Plaza Hotel—where I had been told the Spanish party would meet. They were late, which didn't surprise me, so I hung around and watched the tail of the big Columbus Day parade, which was still going up Fifth Avenue—a policeman said it had been passing since about noon. It was a lovely day, a bit chilly, with clear golden sunlight coming down. The crowd by the avenue seemed rather sparse, and the parade itself to be on the dull side. It was strung out thin, for one thing, which worked against smartness, and it seemed to rely over-much on amateur talent, like school-children. Yet a really good band came by now and then, and almost any show would have been fun in that weather; so I stood and enjoyed it. Then after a while I sat on a stone bench by the flowerbeds. They were full of chrysanthe-mums—yellow, white, maroon, and lavender—which spar-kled in the sunlight and gave out their autumnal smell.

Toward four o'clock I noticed people gathering by a lamp-post near the Park, and I went there and found that they were the Spanish group. There were about two dozen of them, without many Puerto Ricans as yet. Most were men, and except for two or three photographers, they were dressed almost uniformly in the somber clothes that mid-dle-class Spanish-Americans—but not necessarily the Puer-to Rican migrants—seem to favor on public occasions. Some wore overcoats and some wore suits alone, and the latter were almost funereal in their effect. Soon after I joined the group it began moving off. We walked slowly northward beside the drive that enters the Park at that point.

The statue turned out to be at the Mall's south end; it was of green bronze on a granite pedestal, and a few celebrants had reached it before us. They had brought two or three flags and a big wreath, on a tripod, and had leaned three placards against the pedestal's base. The central one read:

WE DO NOT KNOW WHERE
HE WAS BORN BUT WE DO KNOW
HIM AS A CITIZEN OF SPAIN
AND AS THE ADMIRAL
OF THE SPANISH EXPEDITION
IN WHICH THE NEW WORLD
WAS ·FOUNDED

AMERICA WAS DISCOVERED
FOR THE GLORY OF SPAIN
AND THE GOOD OF ALL PEOPLE

The other placards, one in Spanish and one in English, bore out the same theme. They all had stones against their lower edges, but even so they blew over from time to time in the wind. The sunlight was paler now and was slanting at a low angle. The trees by the Mall had lost many of their leaves, and those that remained were turning; but their color was a subdued olive-yellow, rather than bright or golden.

I fell to talking with a slight, dark-haired man in a black suit. He told me that this statue was known as the Spanish Columbus—to distinguish it from the non-Spanish one in Columbus Circle—and that it had been subscribed for by New York's Spanish community in the 'twenties, at the instigation of *La Prensa* and the Spanish-American consulates here.

"Because people were not thinking of Columbus in connection with Spain," he said. "You know how it is here on Columbus Day. Almost every idea is brought in but that of Spain itself."

The statue had been done by a Spanish sculptor, he said, and had been cast in Barcelona; and indeed I found an inscription to this effect on its base, though it gave the date as 1892. My friend couldn't explain the discrepancy; he felt sure the actual erection here had been in the 'twenties, and he didn't know the statue's history before that.

"After it was put up, anyway," he continued, "we had celebrations here every year on Columbus Day, with the consuls of the Spanish Republics taking part. But in the 'thirties this custom was interrupted by the Spanish Civil

War—" he shrugged—"you know what that did to our community. And it is only in the past couple of years that we have begun again."

The wreath-laying was now almost half an hour overdue —it had been scheduled for four—but people were still arriving. Another wreath and another banner arrived too. The latter was green with gold letters and said FEDERACION DE SOCIEDADES HISPANAS INC. I looked again at the group of flags and noted that the two tallest ones were the Stars and Stripes and a replica—so I was told—of the old Castilian pennant under which Columbus had sailed. Its design was handsome—quartered, with two golden castles on red and two red lions rampant on lavender-gray.

The crowd had grown to a few score by now, and several Puerto Ricans had joined it; they could be spotted by their lighter-colored clothes—brighter-colored, indeed, in the case of the women, one of whom wore a shocking-pink coat and another a pale-green one. And suddenly there was a stir, the crowd closed in, and the ceremony began. The speakers, as time went on, included two or three laymen and a priest. I could get only a glimmer of what they said, but it seemed to be on expected lines—about the glories of Spanish culture in the New World, and how everyone should revere it and be guided by it. I didn't pay close attention, but took to loitering outside the crowd, in the fall air and the earthy Park smells.

I did this for some time and then went back to the fringe again. The priest was talking about a return to the old spiritual values of Spain, now that materialism was failing us. Columbus stood on high behind him, and the audience was listening respectfully—perhaps even intently, as if the words were reaching their hearts. The autumn trees by the Mall stood in orderly, parallel rows, and the whole compo-

sion—with the decorous little throng before the statue—
looked somehow like a European scene. I gazed at it and
mused, and as I mused I heard clapping, and the ceremony
was over.

I walked to the East Side IRT, took an uptown local, and
rose again to daylight at 110th and Lexington. The sun had
not yet set, but fell only on the high parts of the buildings
now, and did not reach the sidewalks. The street-scene was
more intimate, I felt at once, than it had been farther down-
town. The buildings were six stories high at most, and many
of them had people on their front steps. Even the crossing
of the street and avenue seemed on a village, not a monu-
mental, scale—the life of the facing sidewalks seemed
joined together, somehow, not parted by fierce traffic as in
midtown.

Many people were out, though I saw no sign that Columbus Day had much to do with this; rather it seemed a case
of Saturday afternoon and good weather. As I walked along
I met girls, now and then, who were already dressed for
the evening—with make-up, flaring skirts, and all—and were
on their way with escorts. I passed men standing everywhere—on sidewalks, on streetcorners—idling and talking
in groups. The bigger boys were playing stickball and the
little ones were spinning tops, throwing them down hard
on the pavement.

I kept walking, and after a while I came to a rubble
wasteland, where a couple of blocks had been torn down
for a housing project. A few buildings were still standing in
it, though, in lonely silence. I saw a fourth-floor window
move mysteriously in one of these; it wagged back and forth
a few times, then disappeared inside. Somebody looting, I
told myself. Then a minute later a Puerto Rican man came

out the front door with the window under his arm, and walked away. He had a carpenter's rule in his hip pocket and looked like an artisan, and I guessed he was adding it to his stock.

Three boys were standing near the building, too, in the rubble, and they were throwing stones up at the windows; they had to throw at the ones on the third floor, though, at some effort, because those on the first and second were too far gone already. Near them stood a sign that read

VACANT LOT
LITTERING
Punishable by
$500
FINE

Yet litter stretched away, amid the rubble, in all directions, and the sign itself seemed the loneliest item in the landscape.

I walked on. I was zigzagging through the area, more or less. I would go east for a block, then south for a block, then west, then south again, and so on. The long crosstown blocks were more residential, on the whole, with more people in them, playing or loitering; the short blocks of the avenues, for their part, had bigger shops, and sights of greater moment. There were several cops around, on the watch for trouble, but they seemed on the whole to be single—not patrolling in pairs.

I threaded my way through the people, young and old, and the marks of their Puerto Rican origin seemed everywhere. Even the pavements bore them, for I kept finding shreds there of the husk of sugar-cane, which the people had been chewing, as they do on the island. The whole scene had the warmth of humanity in it, and even the buildings—red brick or brownstone, as a rule—were warm and soft in texture. Above them the sky was still azure. Once, looking up there, I saw an odd sight—a dummy hanging on a rope that had been stretched across the street, from one cornice to another. It was made of a plaid shirt and some old gray trousers that had been stuffed, and it looked macabre against the blue sky. I stopped and asked some young men what it represented, and they said it was a Yankee put there by some Braves fans—this was soon after the World Series—but whether they spoke the truth I could not tell.

Another time, while walking down Madison Avenue, I saw a wedding group in a tiny photo-shop. There were eight or ten in the group, and they filled the place entirely. The bride was lovely, and she had a long satin train and a white fur stole. The bridesmaids—one of whom was almost blonde—wore blue dresses. The flower-girl seemed no more than three feet high, but she wore lipstick as well as a blue crocheted scarf, a flaring skirt, and what I have since been told was a halo of white tulle set back on the head. There was a page-boy too, of about the same size, and in company with the groom and best man he wore a black tie, black evening-trousers, and white jacket, the last rather zootish in cut.

The party made a handsome sight, and the walls of the little shop were hung with pictures of similar wedding-groups. I felt that this photo-ceremony must be a main step in the wedding-procedure of El Barrio—coming after the church, perhaps, and before a reception. And I noted that a car, a sedan with a pink streamer, was waiting by the curb as if to bear the couple onward.

In my rambling I avoided Third and Fifth Avenues, by and large, for they were on the fringes of the Puerto Rican district. This meant that I walked alternately on Park and Lexington or Park and Madison. Park differed from the other two in having the railway over it. Below 111th Street the rails were on a massive stone viaduct, pierced by the cross-streets, but from 111th to 116th they had a public market underneath them—enclosed, for the length of each block, by sheet-iron, painted green. There were many open stalls on the sidewalks too, especially on the western ones. These were selling everything—clothes, toys, Puerto Rican foodstuffs—and I gazed at them with interest as I passed. I noted, among other things, that much warm clothing was on sale now, with the winter coming.

Then once, while thus engaged, I saw a quick dramatic incident. I was going up the western sidewalk toward an intersection, when suddenly a boy came running from the closed-in market-space ahead of me, with another older, stockier man in close pursuit. The man caught him and punched him, knocking him down in the street, then turned and walked back toward the market-place. The boy got up and leaned against a car, holding his chin and, I thought, sobbing; and two friends appeared to comfort him. The man, who wore a white sweatshirt and looked like a welterweight boxer, kept walking back toward the market, and as he drew near it a woman standing there cried "Shame!" at him. "Shame?" he answered. "You wouldn't say that if you'd seen what he did. He was stealing." And he stalked inside. Meanwhile the boy had pulled himself together, and he walked off with his two friends. I went into the market and found the man behind a stall there, putting away the last of some fruit he had had on display. "What was the boy doing?" I asked. "He was stealing," the man said tersely and defensively. "He was stealing, and he won't steal again."

The sky bore a hint of dusk now, and I decided to call on a leading citizen of El Barrio, a certain Pedro Canino, of whom I had often heard and whom I had met once, briefly, while visiting PS 108, the show-place school at 108th Street and Madison Avenue. Canino's home was near the school, I found, on looking in the phone-book—it was at 20 East 109th, which turned out to be a relatively well-kept building of walk-up apartments; the halls were decently plastered, and newly painted in light blue. Canino's place was on the third floor, and luckily I found him in—he opened the door after a moment's delay.

He recognized me almost at once, and motioned me in cordially. He was a well-set-up, handsome, vigorous man, with broad shoulders and broad hands that gave a firm handshake. He was wearing a double-breasted blue suit, a white shirt, and a dark-blue tie with white polka dots. He began talking at once. He spoke expressive English with very little accent, but his ideas came out in a hot torrent that was hard to follow.

"I have just been out in the hinterland myself," he said. "I was getting a shopping-bag for a family of thirteen. The father is just out of the hospital, you know, and they are going to be evicted. Oh, I am always broke." He struck his forehead with his palm. "But somebody has to feed them."

He showed me to an armchair in the front room and sat down on a small sofa himself. The room was nicely furnished, with a kitchen table, straight chairs, a radio, a television set, and a bookshelf full of books. There was a kitchenette in the corner toward the rear, and on the table by it I noticed some oranges in what looked like a tinfoil frozen-pie container.

I didn't take all these details in at first, though, because Mr. Canino didn't let my attention wander long enough. "You can't imagine the poverty," he said. "These factory owners and what not, they fasten themselves like leeches on the Puerto Ricans. Forty-five dollars a week is average wage for Puerto Ricans, you know. Forty-five dollars. Think of it. And for some miserable little room they must pay sixteen, eighteen. How can they live?"

I started to ask a question, but he eluded me, and before I knew it he was talking about a "poor woman who had to have an operation, and it was done at home." She had been cheated, apparently, but whether by the doctor, the hospital, or the union to which she had been paying benefit fees, I could not make out. Nor could I cross-examine my host, for he had the conversation in hand himself, and he rushed ahead with feeling and expression.

Suddenly he was telling me about a landlord who had made "forty-five wretched pigeonholes out of five apartments. Forty-five of them, can you believe it? Renting for sixteen, eighteen, twenty-three dollars. Nine hundred dollars a week he is making. More than that. Can you imagine it? And he has put in nothing. Nothing."

Mr. Canino made strong, sweeping, graceful gestures with his hands, and his eyes flashed, and his white teeth gleamed. He had a handsome, well-shaped head with graying hair, and I felt that in any society he would have become a leader of some sort, with his vigor and eloquence, and his feeling for the people.

"The law of evidence is no good if between Americans and Puerto Ricans," he was suddenly saying. "Often there is unfair translation in the courts, and even without this there is usually no understanding. You cannot say what's in your heart"—and he clasped his two hands to his breast. "You can only say yes or no. And for a Puerto Rican, that is putting you in a strait-jacket."

As he talked a knock sounded at the door, and a smallish woman came from the rear of the apartment to open it. She let in a nice-looking, healthy boy in his early teens. Both of them came forward, and Mr. Canino introduced them as his wife and son. The wife—a pretty woman, though no longer young—merely said hello, and then withdrew to the rear again; but the boy stayed on to talk with his father a moment. He spoke excellent English, and he asked if the father had told the landlord not to let him and some friends use a certain room in a neighboring basement for club sessions.

"Yes, I did tell him that," the father answered. "I want you to use the room, but not without supervision, and so I told him not to let you in there till this could be arranged."

He spoke tenderly, and the boy took the ruling quietly and respectfully. He was wearing a white sweatshirt with the insignia of Hunter College on it, and he told me he had gotten this from his sister, who was a Hunter graduate. The father added that these two were his only children. His daughter had studied in Puerto Rico awhile after graduating from Hunter, and she was now teaching at PS 108. The son, for his part, had just finished at PS 108 and was now going, with the help of a scholarship, to the City and Country School on West 12th Street. Canino said thankfully that this was a great break, and I felt it was a well-deserved one, too, for I had rarely seen a more prepossessing boy.

He left, and before his father could start on something else I asked when he had come up here from Puerto Rico.

"In 1925," he said. "I was a young man then, but I could speak English—I had been teaching school down on the island. First I went to work as a steamfitter here, but I wasn't strong enough. I couldn't take it. I went out on a job in Queens in the wintertime. It was very cold, and I was working on a furnace; there was water in the basement, and I fell in it—twice I fell in it, and I got a cramp in my stomach, and had to quit."

He rolled his eyes and made a tragic face. "Then I got a job in the post office, and I have been there ever since. I am a timekeeper now, though I have done all kinds of things. I have done translating and interpreting—everything—but officially I am a timekeeper. It is hard to rise beyond that."

I had been told more than once of a rent clinic that Mr. Canino helped to run, and I asked him about this. "Yes," he said. "It is called rent clinic, but that's a misnomer really. We do everything. Everything." And he was off again.

"Now we have a Civic Orientation Center," he said. "Is in a miserable little basement room that we fixed up ourselves. We help with rent problems—they are the worst—but we help with welfare and other things too. Everybody comes. They all have problems, and they don't know what to do."

He shook his head. "The thing that's closest to my heart," he said, "is an office at street level. An office at street level with two stenographers. If we had that we could do everything."

He began talking about some housing abuses he had been fighting, and once more I had trouble in following him. The cases were complex, and he went from one to another with dizzying speed. He mentioned a Puerto Rican landlord who had evicted his tenants in wintertime—"threw them all out in the snow, and they were his own country-

men." Then he was suddenly talking about another landlord, not a Puerto Rican, who had sold some old buildings
to the city and then bought them back again, in a way that
smacked of skulduggery. And then he was on a third case,
in which a landlord had made a fake sale, to a dummy
corporation, which had legally enabled him, somehow, to
evict his tenants and take in a set of new ones, at the same
rents plus a new "sale" fee for each of them—"and you can
sell the lousiest apartment here for two hundred, three
hundred dollars," Mr. Canino said.

He had been waging ceaseless war against such landlords, I gathered, and had called in powerful help on occasion. He had had correspondence with Alfred E. Sant-
angelo, the congressman of the district, and with Bernice
Rogers of the Department of Buildings, and had even been
to see Mayor Wagner—he seemed to have reasonably good
access to the Mayor, who had been supported more solidly
by voters in East Harlem, he said, than in any other part of
the city. I could easily imagine Mr. Canino pleading with
these officials, or bombarding them with letters, till his
energy swept them into action.

Yet he was paying a price for it all, he said, through a
heart ailment that had begun to trouble him. The doctor
had been telling him to take it easy. "But what can I do?"
he asked me. "I have my own work on top of all this, and I
can't stop it. I have to eat. It's a must." And he threw his
hands upward in a gesture.

I asked him if I could see his basement center, and he
said "Certainly," already getting up. "It's a miserable place,
and I hope you will forgive it, but you are certainly welcome to have a look." And he ushered me out the door and
down the stairs.

We reached the sidewalk, turned east, and began a sort of

royal progress down the block, for we kept meeting people whom Mr. Canino knew and had some business with—he would promise to fix something for them, or would ask them to do some work at the center, or would merely pass the time of day. He talked English with them when he could, partly for my benefit, I gathered, and partly out of principle. "It's so important for these people to learn English, and practice it," he said. "A while ago I made a trip back to Puerto Rico, and when I was there I kept saying it from the treetops, that they *must* learn English if they were coming here."

We walked along, and one of the people we met was Mr. Canino's daughter, on her way home from somewhere. She too was healthy and pleasant-looking, and she wore a jacket-sweater-blouse-and-skirt ensemble that struck me as typical of American girls in their twenties. We had a few words with her and then passed on.

The center was a block away to the south. It was down a cramped flight of stairs from the sidewalk, and a small sign over its door read CIVIC ORIENTATION CENTER INC. It was closed at that late hour on Saturday, but Mr. Canino unlocked the door and led me in. The room was a plain one, but neat, and furnished with two old desks, half a dozen straight chairs, a table, and an old wooden filing-cabinet.

I remarked how clean the place was. "Yes," he said, "we do the best we can, but it's pretty hard." And he pointed to the floor behind me. "Look," he said. I looked, and a cockroach was invading us through a crack beneath a door— apparently from some other basement room. The cockroach came out into the open, then another followed it, and then a third; and the three of them scooted round till Mr. Canino stepped on them. "You can see what we are up against," he said, and he began talking again about a room at street-level with two paid stenographers—he had part-time volunteer ones now, he explained, but they never could be counted on; they would come home tired from their jobs, and that would be the end of it, and you really couldn't blame them.

He took me over to the filing-cabinet and began showing me some letters—about devious housing cases, for the most part, and I didn't study them closely. But he also had some photographs of steam radiators, which he said were against the regulations, and these were easier to take in. Some of them were only two sections wide, and without valves to turn them off.

"Look at them," he said. "By 1958 every multiple dwelling in New York must have central heating. And when a landlord puts it in he can raise the rent by four dollars. So this is what they do. But the tenants can't control these things, and they will roast. See this one. It is only four feet from the bed, so the place is unlivable. And you see where the pipe comes out of the wall." He pointed, and it was coming out of a ragged hole in the plaster. "They tore that hole there five, six months ago and still haven't filled it in, so the rats can walk through any time they want. Oh, you wouldn't believe how these people are exploited. And unless we get the facts the city will do nothing."

He put the photos back and we rose to the street again and made a little tour, Mr. Canino showing me through a few nearby flats, which were much like those I had seen in the colder weather: overcrowded, poorly furnished, and with lots of children running round—and usually with TV sets as well. I asked him about the family of thirteen that was about to be evicted—which he had mentioned at the beginning of my visit—and he said he would take me there; the house had one of the worst landlords in the section. So

we set out for it, and it happened to be in the block where
I had earlier seen the dummy hanging. It was still there,
too, though against a darker sky by now, and I asked Mr.
Canino what it signified.

"I don't know," he said, "but it ought to be the landlord.
He is a real crook. He doesn't visit his buildings here much,
but he squeezes them dry. He puts nothing into them, and
he takes a fortune out, and if the tenants get behind in rent
he throws them into the street. Even if their wives are
having babies he throws them there—even if they are right
in the middle of it."

The family of thirteen was in a long apartment, with a
kitchen in the rear and small living-room in the front, and
between them a strung-out passageway that seemed to be
all of one piece, though I suppose it was technically divided
into separate chambers. This passage was lined on one side
by double-decker bunks, and there were children everywhere, more or less knee high. In the front room two or
three young men—guests, I took it—were looking at a Western on a small TV set, and the elders of the family were
gathered in the kitchen, sitting there gloomily—demoral-
ized, I felt, by Nueva York in general, as well as by the
husband's illness. They had the windows tight shut, and
the air in the place was already warm and close, with what
seemed like the cooking smells of many days.

We stayed there but a moment, and on leaving we were
accosted by a woman in the hall; she had seen us entering
from across the street and had come over expressly to tell
me—in perfect New York English, it turned out—about the
landlord's misdemeanors.

"Come upstairs," she said, "and I will show you a great
hole in the ceiling of a bathroom, above the toilet, that has
been there for weeks. The landlord won't fix it because he

hasn't found the tin yet. He never does anything till he finds some tin around."

She led us upstairs and knocked at a door, but no one answered. "They are out," she said. "It's too bad. But the hole is as big as that." And she held her hands two or three feet apart. "Isn't it, Pedro?"

Canino nodded, and we started down the stairs again. Big patches of the wall were bare of plaster. "He won't fix those till he learns that the inspector is coming," the woman said. "Then do you know what he does? He puts newspapers in the holes and throws a little plaster on them. Of course it all falls out again in a few days, but meanwhile the inspector has seen it."

We went back down to the sidewalk, and I saw that the building had a row of basement windows without panes, and with old, ill-fitting scraps of metal in their place. "You see, he's found the tin for that," the woman said, contemptuously. "It took him a long time, but he's a patient man. He can wait forever till some tin shows up."

It was really dark now, so I took leave of Mr. Canino and the woman and went back to my wandering. People were still out on the sidewalks, but they were fewer and more warmly dressed, for the air was getting cold. Twice I passed women with babies, and the babies were cocooned in blankets beyond recognition.

I saw one more trace of violence: a boy writhing on the sidewalk and clutching at his leg. He writhed there all alone, though people were passing, till he managed to stand up and hobble off. Some women were sitting in a parked car right beside him, but they were minding their own business. When the boy had limped away I went and asked them what it was all about, but they didn't answer me. Then a well-dressed man came up to their car, and I asked him. "Oh, it is part of that gang business," he said quietly. "You know what I mean. Now perhaps he has gone to get some of *his* gang, and they will hurt the boys who hurt him. I wonder how it all can ever end." And he got into the car and drove it off.

Farther down that street, at a corner, I came on a revivalist preacher. He was a dark, wiry little man, with gray hair and an overcoat, and in his right hand he held a length of rough twine with a noose in the end of it. He would bend over and lay the noose down on the pavement, talking a blue streak in Spanish about the devil's wiles, and then would pretend to walk his left hand carelessly into it. The right hand would pull the noose tight, and the left would be caught fast for all its struggling, while the old man preached on the entrapments of sin, and the crowd listened appreciatively.

I walked on, and the shop-windows were still more appealing now, lit up in the darkness. Some of the food shops had red neon silhouettes of pigs in their windows, advertising *lechón asado,* or roast pork, which is a great Puerto Rican delicacy. Not a few shop-fronts were finished in aluminum or chromium—sometimes with red lettering—in a bright, gay style that seemed to give those modern metals a special Puerto Rican look. I thought the shops seemed fairly prosperous, too, and I got the vague impression that El Barrio's living standards had risen since the winter before.

Not all the shops were open, of course, but it was fun to look in the closed ones, too. I noted a window that was displaying religious objects—not to mention superstitious ones. It had images of Christ and the Virgin along with

pictures of some Hindu deities, including Shiva, the De-
stroyer, and Hanuman, the Monkey God, and, down at the
bottom, a pamphlet entitled *Policy Pete's Mutuel Number
Dream Book* was leaning against the other things. It had
a picture of an owl on it, with the admonition "Be Wise,"
and it was priced at twenty-five cents.

I wandered on, and in time I had my fill of El Barrio and
decided to go elsewhere for the evening. Before leaving,
though, I went into a nice, brightly-lit *bodega* and bought
a can each of *papaya* juice, *guanábana* juice, *tamarind* juice,
guava shells, and *mango* slices, all packed in Puerto Rico.
They came to $1.48 together.

I hailed a cab and set out for the Caborrojeño, a dance-
hall at Broadway and 146th Street. This is in the Washington Heights section, north of Columbia, and I had walked
around there somewhat the previous spring—it is a spacious, airy part of town, with houses and apartment buildings still in good repair; and for the Puerto Ricans who
live there—along with Negroes and others—it is a good step
upward from their poorer ghettos. The Caborrojeño was
on the second floor of its building—up a narrow, carpeted
flight of stairs and past a ticket window—and the festivities
were well under way when I arrived.

I found a table near the dance floor and ordered beer
and *pasteles*—a Puerto Rican delicacy, long like an *en-
chilada,* and made of steamed meat and cereals. The dance-
floor was bigger than a full-size tennis court, and its low
ceiling was covered, in the part near the orchestra, by
festoons of yellow cloth, which deadened the sound a
little, but not much. Two or three hundred people were in
the place, either dancing or sitting at tables, and they were

being indulgently supervised by three or four bouncers dressed in blue uniforms with patches on their arms saying FACTFINDERS DETECTIVE BUREAU.

The orchestra, at the back of the room, was a big one of a dozen pieces, and these seemed well chosen; there were four saxophones and three horns, plus three sets of drums, a piano, a bass viol, and now and then a pair of *maracas*. The bass was the only stringed instrument among them, technically, and it really functioned as percussion. The noise they put out seemed all blare and rhythm. After I sat down, a *rhumba* started, and the four saxophonists, who were all in a row, stood up and waved their hips in time to it, while playing. Then my beer and *pasteles* came, and after a while the four saxes withdrew from the room, leaving the other pieces in charge.

The Caborrojeño, I soon began to realize, was much more purely Spanish than the Palladium, on Broadway and 53rd Street, the other big Puerto Rican night-spot that I knew. There were virtually no jazz rhythms in the Caborrojeño's music, for one thing. Again, the announcements here were in Spanish, not in English like the Palladium's. Information about the dances was given in Spanish on a public-address system, often in a girl's voice, and so were paging messages—"*Que venga Tony Rodriguez al telefon*," the girl would say, and things like that. Finally, the crowd here was much more Spanish in its looks than the motley one at the Palladium. There were a few non-Spanish young people around, who I thought might be Columbia students, but the vast majority of people were Puerto Ricans.

They were fair-skinned Puerto Ricans, by and large. I noted one big dark woman, in a lavender dress, dancing amiably with a middle-aged, fair-skinned Puerto Rican man who had sideburns that looked like bowie knives, but she was an exception. Nearly everyone in the room was pale—pale and well dressed—and I wondered if a high-grade Puerto Rican community, a sort of cotillion set, was developing here on the Upper West Side.

I had another beer, and the music went on, dance after dance. Sometimes there would be a loud-singing *plena*. Then a *merengue* would blare out, really sending the place —filling it with molten gold, so to speak, and firelight. The orchestra had its sweet, soft styles as well, and it played these often, but somehow they didn't change the picture much. After a while the four saxophones came back to the room, and then the music was still brassier.

The dancing itself was more staid, I reflected—more genteel—than at the Palladium. Most of the girls wore good, and even expensive-looking, evening-dresses—one girl that I noted, for instance, had on a cream-colored, slit-down-the-back job that looked almost as if it had come from Fifth Avenue. Their partners seemed sophisticated, too, in the courtesy or ritual of their dancing; they acted far more suavely to each other, I felt, than mainlanders would act. And regardless of their dress, the girls usually had a faraway, detached look once they got out on the floor. They would do the most intricate, fantastic things with their feet, but meanwhile their expressions would be other-worldly. They would also chew gum, even the most chic of them—it seemed an integral part of their performance. And finally they seemed, almost without exception, to have greater stature while dancing than while at rest. When the music stopped and they headed back for their tables, they straightway seemed less dignified, somehow, less significant, and even smaller.

I drank more beer and looked at the nearby tables. Much of the dancing was on a pick-up basis, it seemed, with the house-cops looking on benignly. Some tables had groups of four girls at them, and even more had groups of four men. They would sit there talking, and a man would rise, now and then, and ask a girl to dance. I also found a row of girls sitting, like wall flowers, at the chamber's far end, by the washrooms. A crowd of men, a formless stag-line, milled about near by; often one would ask a girl to dance, and she might answer yes or no.

The evening wore on, and by eleven the place was jammed with people and full of hot, stale air. The customers were getting deeper in the mood. A man at the table next to me was beating on a glass with a knife, in beery approximation of the rhythm. A house-cop—rather fat— came by and remonstrated with him, leaning over in a friendly, meddlesome way. The man stopped banging till he left, then started up again. I had had quite a few beers myself by now, and I felt it was time to go home, so I rose and started for the exit. But when I reached it, I took a last backward look. The place seemed filled with its dense, hard noise, the percussion beating and the brass giving out its blary warmth. The people were in a milling, flailing throng—making lots of motion, but not much progress. They seemed like fish swimming happily in some element unfamiliar to me. They seemed full of the music. It seemed to live in them, and they in it. And pondering this I headed down the stairs.